CW01639518

# FELICITY KEATS

DANCING PENCILS

First Edition

Published by
umSinsi Press
PO Box 28129
MALVERN
4055
KwaZulu Natal
Republic of South Africa

Tel: +27-31 4641556

ISBN 1-86900-163-X

Web: http://www.umsinsi.com

# FELICITY KEATS

DANCING PENCILS

## CONTENTS

## PART THREE: THE OUTSIDE STORY, FROM INSIDE

# ACKNOWLEDGEMENTS

The acknowledgements to this book are so many that I barely know where to start. My thanks go to every one of my many students and all those that I have *ever* met personally or otherwise. You have *all* added something to the growth of this book.

# DANCING PENCILS

## PART ONE: THE CREATIVE PROCESS

### Chapter 1: Introduction to Part One

Writing is shrouded in mystery and confusion. I remember long ago asking a successful author how to write a book - because that's what I wanted to do.

She airily waved her hand and said, "It's like the lily. It just grows and blooms."

Maybe that's how the writing happens that I now do myself and how the writing happens for the many others that I teach and have taught. But at least I can tell you how to propagate that plant and bring the flowers forth, so that you know that you *can* write, whatever you would like to write.

Please note that this book is more for insights and unlocking of the right brain than it is for exact techniques; and it is divided into three sections.

The first section concerns the creative process and how to access the right brain.

The second section shows you how to use the right brain for the various genres, using a non-traditional approach. There are also examples of excellent work, some in its raw state, some of it already published, from just a few students. This section also looks at how I run different workshops for adults, teachers or children, in the various fields of writing.

The third section is an inside story of our successes, children and adults, some of whom have gone on to become international authors.

## Chapter 2: Dancing Pencils

A feeling of wonder, of amazement and of harmony fills me as I look at a sea of dancing pencils. There have been as many as two hundred heads bent low over their papers, the pencils moving rapidly, to total silence - or to perhaps the soft background sound of classical music such as Handel, Mozart, Vivaldi. Most of the time, groups are much smaller. Sometimes, just one person alone is learning creative right-brained writing.

Strangely, it is possible to tell when the learners have entered a right-brained or creative state. Something shifts in the atmosphere. Something imperceptible, but there comes a moment when I *know* they have shifted and are writing creatively. The body language is different. There is a fluidity, a harmony of body, mind and spirit, with just the quiet dancing pencils moving over the unlined paper.

For we use books without lines. Unlined paper, because lines get in the way of the right brain which works best without restraints of any kind. And books of paper - because pieces of paper can too easily be rolled up and thrown away. Or lost. This kind of writing is far too good for that. It is the writing of the soul, and it is the writing from which come the germs of poems, of novels, or of deep thought. Characters are born, along with a passion for writing which leads to a love of reading.

Because this is the world of the imagination and creativity, and it is a case of getting over to the right brain, to the place where resides the noble part of man or woman. It is by writing with this part of a person, in the timeless zone of creativity, unified with the whole of the universe, that great work is produced. For this right-brained writing cannot overwrite. It cannot pick the wrong adjective and the language used is better than the thinking left-brain could come up with.

Not that I am discounting the left brain. We need a *whole*

brain. That is the aim. But society is geared towards the left brain, towards study and doing well and rewarding students that fit this category: who conform.

Using a whole brain gives the best results but before we get to that stage, let us primarily look at the ways in which to unlock and to release the powers held dormant in the right brain.

Might I mention, though, that I wrote for many years without bothering about which part of my brain I was using. I just knew that sometimes it went better than others. Sometimes I would look at a blank piece of paper and nothing would come.

We accepted there was such a thing as writers' block. We accepted that there were periods of silence when writers had said all that was in them, or for some reason of their own, had turned from words to some other creative medium. Paint, for instance. Or to drama.

When the choice is conscious that is fine. But when there is a deep longing in the soul to write, and for some reason the person *can't* write, then it's time to take a look at the right brain, at its powers, and how to unlock it and to access it, and to work with it as your partner, as you move towards whole-brained writing.

I speak with the knowledge of someone who has been there. I have had this tug-of-war throughout my life, with writing demanding that I make room for it. Make choices, change things, live a different way, work hard, do things I never thought of doing, and that I'd never planned, as I pirouetted to the tune of my dancing pencil.

I speak of many years of freelance journalism. Good years, yet years in which the desire to write fiction clawed at my insides and demanded to be let out. It wasn't easy to change over from journalism to fiction. The mind is such a delicate and yet such a powerful tool. Once when I was getting nicely into writing fiction, I programmed myself not to write at all. How could this happen?

I was asked to write an article, which needed research, for a magazine. I didn't want to do it, was having fun practising fiction techniques. Then, feeling guilty about the article, I wrote a note to myself. *No more writing fiction until that article is done.*

The article continued to be shunted to the back, and then I found that all my writing ability had gone. Why couldn't I write? I wondered.

Then one day I found the note. *No more writing fiction until that article is done.*

Illumination beamed down on me. I got stuck into that article just as soon as I could and decided then that I would pass on any article writing I was asked to do, to other people equipped to help, so that I could keep my small bit of free time available for my precious fiction writing.

## Chapter 3: You are important

That brings me to a vital point. You are important. We are all important. We matter. In fact, each of us is the most important person in our lives. We need to be honest, to discover that for ourselves, and then to admit it. I know this because for so much of my life I found that I was not doing things that mattered to me because others had become more important in my life than I.

This idea may cause horror to people, but I spent many years considering this question. After much reading I came to find that it was true that if all people did what they really and truly loved best and put their needs right at the top, then they could be wonderfully giving and caring for the rest of the time: they would have inner peace and contentment. That means a writer needs to find space and time to write. I will come to all of that later on.

First, it needs a decision, an inner knowing, that: *I am a writer.* Next comes a very important counter problem. How am I to make a living?

Because, paradoxically, if a writer thinks of money, the writing won't be so good. Or, if it is good, it isn't actually what the writer really wants to write. So maybe another way of earning a living that doesn't entirely consume the person's time might be the answer. You need to understand the choices, and that ripples come from choices that can turn into waves and even breakers that could drown you. So - be careful when you are deciding how to live out your dream. Because you might become too busy.

When this happens, the quality of life deteriorates. There is no time left to smell the roses, to see a bird in the sky or the clouds that are building up for rain after a dry period. No time to live the two lives that I tell writers about: the one is the ordinary life we all live.

The second life that goes along simultaneously with the

first is the ability of the artist and writer within to see things exactly as they are, in that moment. To experience the rain as it hits the dust, to see the shine of the moon on a lake, to feel the drip of cold rain down one's neck and to experience it, to know it, as something more real than just getting wet in the rain.

It is this living twice, this being in the moment, this caring about people and what happens, and how different people react in different ways, without making judgements about right and wrong, that is the writer's storehouse and treasury.

In a way, of which I have no understanding, the creative unconscious, your writing muse, or whoever or whatever it is that helps you (William Blake says that it is God) when you are truly writing as a creative artist, with every bit of your fibre on what you are creating, that appropriate bits of what you have seen, done and experienced at any point of your lives somehow become woven into your work in a most exciting way. You could never have *thought* this up and put it in a piece of worked-out prose. But I will explain this at a later point in this book.

For now I am talking of you being important. And if you want to write, if there is a longing inside of you, or if you have in your care, others who have this desire, this book will help you to release that creative spirit without damaging it. For it is fragile and very easily destroyed. You will get to understand all of this as you proceed with me through the pages of this book.

## Chapter 4: Belief

The second point to make after giving yourself value, of saying, *I matter, this is my choice, and I am going to find a way, and time, to write,* is that of belief. Belief is of fundamental importance.

There was a book I read at the very moment when I most needed to. It was called *The Magic of Believing* by Claude M. Bristol. And it made some very important observations: it talked of healing which was done in various parts of the world with different kinds of people. And the author came to the conclusion that it was the beliefs of these people that brought about the results for each group.

Further along in the book, he touched on the importance of word pictures in getting belief implanted into a person's being. He gave a description of a firm in difficulties which had a management meeting at which it asked members to draw in word picture form what material possessions they would like to have, and to make four copies of this word picture and to put them in strategic places where they would see them during the day.

This is giving your right brain a mind picture for it to create a belief and so, unexpectedly one would open a drawer, or one's wallet, and get a reminder of this need or dream. The author went on to say that he later met people from that meeting, who by bringing about new beliefs about themselves had acquired exactly what they had written, that day.

As the right brain is the side that works and thinks in pictures, I took this further. In the field of advertising, a car that aims to appeal to the right brain shows the car in picture form, whilst a car for the left brain has a lot of written description about it. It is the picture that will sell the car and not the words; the words justify the decision.

After reading Claude M. Bristol's book, and long before I became an author, at a time when I never believed I could write a book that would be published, I drew pictures of people buying my books and loving them. I drew pictures and forgot I'd done it.

Every so often, I find these pictures and I smile. At the time I had the desire but not the belief. Now I have both the desire and the belief. I also know that what I have found out in my lifetime of writing that I am sharing with others in this book, really works, and that this book, too, will prove that belief is a vital part in the process of writing, and of the development of writers.

Because writing as a lifetime's work is not easy. "The gold in them thar hills," beckons. Dreams of becoming millionaires from books made into films must be high on the list of many people who toil at jobs that they really don't like, and who have an artist within demanding that they do something about giving it a chance.

From experience again, I would say it is better to work at something that puts the food on the table and pays the rent and then to be able to make choices that give time for writing, than to throw everything overboard and go off to write that best seller. Some people do just that, and they make it happen, but that's the minority.

If you believe, and if you stick to your belief and keep focussed you will achieve your dreams. But remember always, aim for the stars and you'll reach the moon. A tiny goal the size of a mole-hill might give you an even tinier result which would hardly be exciting.

The mind again is so powerful.

Again, in dealing with belief, an important strategy is to start at the top, and see a project as finished, and then to start at the bottom and proceed to make it happen.

I have heard many variants of this story: one is of the great violin maestro who took his seven-year old pupil to the stage to take a bow before a huge empty auditorium. That was before the child even put bow to violin. He was saying to his belief side, or unconscious creative, "I'm going to be so good that I'm going to take a bow here one day."

A similar story exists in the books of Buddhism. An artist was once asked, by the reigning Abbot of Myoshinji, to paint a picture of a dragon. The artist complained, agonized, "But I haven't ever seen a dragon."

"Then become one," said the Abbot. And the artist did, with the resulting applauded work of a marvellous realistic painting of a dragon.

So it is with a book. At some stage, somewhere near the beginning, it is good to see the book finished, completed, bound, being sold, and being positively received. This belief of the book's ability to do what the author wants it to do makes the writing flow along so easily. There is a difference between looking at fifty thousand words and wondering where they are going to come from, and seeing the book *done*. Then it's much easier to starting at the beginning, with the fifty thousand words pouring in a huge stream to make the book very soon a reality.

In Lucia Capacchione's book, *The Power of Your Other Hand,* she made a similar point when she invited Pamela to join her in a television show she was hosting and producing.

But Pamela was petrified and afraid of doing badly. So, with her pen in her non-dominant hand (we are coming to all of this) she drew a picture of herself on television, and looking nervous. She drew the picture again, in a happy frame of mind, and her non-dominant hand wrote "*ON AND DOING FINE.*" That picture went into her mind and that is exactly what happened. She went on the show, smiling, and did do well.

Another idea in belief is given to us in *Writing On Both Sides Of The Brain* by Henriette Anne Klauser when she tells of how she needed to write a really good article that would double as a flyer and as a poster. She just couldn't get it sounding right, so she closed her eyes and "saw" in her imagination, people crowding up to read it as she was tacking it up on bulletin boards in various places. They were smiling and eager to be booked onto her course.

When in her imagination they had all moved off, she went over and read the words that had excited them so much. And as she read them, she wrote them down. She said, it was almost cheating.

I have tried this method myself and have been told the resulting letter which I was having such difficulty in writing, was excellent. Again I had seen it in my imagination. But don't take what you write down as the final finished product. Do some editing, clean it up so that it is grammatically correct and reads well. This way you can get an excellent result, whole-brained and creative, with the corrections done by an agreeable co-operative left brain.

## Chapter 5: The Left Brain

There are huge differences between the left and right brains.

By now, I have taught thousands and thousands of children and adults, and in every case the person has had success using my method. This has thrilled me, and many authors and writers have been fledged. All this has given me time to wonder.

What is it that actually happens? What is the difference between working in the way people are taught in schools and in education colleges, and in working with right-brained creativity?

Let me see if I can put right-brained experiences into left-brained words.

The left brain is the home of thought. It is also the place of learning, and of thinking. It is the place of acquired knowledge and as it grows better and better at acquiring and making use of knowledge, it becomes more opinionated and arrogant. It is a controller and loves to be in control. It also *tries*, and this *trying* implies that it can fail. This is what causes panic with students who want, or need, to do well.

The left brain, then, is looked at as one's critic. One's Caliban. The one who says you can do better. The one who thinks your work is not so good.

Your left brain is meddlesome; it is opinionated. It doesn't wait to see or to understand properly, and often jumps in with assumptions as it thinks it knows everything. Particularly in the case of teachers (of which I am one, myself, please note) the critic has become finely tuned to be on the look-out for errors. It sees things that are *wrong*. It criticizes, analyses and divides. The left brain is also the home of the ego.

Lawyers, accountants, architects and even excellent secretaries have highly developed left brains. These are very necessary in their line of work, and sometimes it is exceedingly hard for this kind of person to move over to a right-brained mode.

To new smallish adult workshops, I often give out pieces of paper folded into three, length-wise, and ask them to write, rapidly and without thinking, fourteen things they feel about themselves. They use the dominant hand for this exercise. I then distract them and talk about other things.

We next come to the part that causes a laugh and disclaimers from many. "Please turn the paper over. Now, using your non-dominant hand, write fourteen things you feel about yourself. Never mind what you wrote first, just write a new list."

When they have finished, they flap the lists over so that both are visible and run their eyes down the lists.

"Tell me if there are any differences," I say. "Big differences, I mean."

In many cases the hands write the same things, but often there are surprises. "You're not reaching your potential," one student wrote with the non-dominant hand. Often the non-dominant hand has generous things to say whilst the dominant hand is critical. This is symbolic of how we mould ourselves to fit the world as it needs us to be.

It's fine to do our job well, as long as we give space to the true side of ourselves, the one that the non-dominant hand taps into. For this is our true self. Often we don't know ourselves and get great shocks as we find ourselves on a course that fits the world but which is quite different from what we really wanted to be or to do. This often means that people are far from reaching any meaningful potential.

As a wonderful exercise, work through Lucia Capacchione's book, *The Power of Your Other Hand*, where your only opponent is yourself, and get to know yourself through dialogue between your dominant and non-dominant hands. I had great fun when I did these exercises, especially as I observed my critic ticking off my creative side, which grew stronger and more confident and then put the critic (my left brain) in its place.

To return to the left brain.

By writing with thought, one is actually separating the audience from the experience you are writing about. Perhaps students who have the most difficulty are highly qualified language teachers. I discovered this when I was running my course in creative writing over a period of four weeks. In lesson two I did *characters*. The first exercise was one character, written about creatively. It was at this point that my very highly educated student read out her character sketch. The words were excellent and so were the descriptions but the image created was fuzzy. I couldn't *see* her character. Writers are told, "If you can't see it yourself in your mind, don't expect your readers to see it either."

I had to explain to her that left-brained writing might be grammatically correct and sound good, but the imaginative work of the right brain is necessary to create literature. As I explained this to her she rather gloomily said that she had just seen now why it was so hard for matriculation students to write their English essays. But once she understood this need for the imagination to be part of the creative process she went on to become a remarkably good writer, and published author, herself.

Whilst famous writers, poets and authors create work that lives forever, probably without bothering about rules or right or left brains, most writers are taught to do work which requires structure. They are taught the way to use language. They understand sentence construction, and syntax. They learn to build their work up to a climax; they think up characters, and learn the use of dialogue and know the proper techniques to use in story writing. The left brain needs to think up plots and backgrounds. It may get a story idea and then fit the ingredients of character, background and plot together. It may find an end and then think of how to get the beginning, the background and the characters.

This, the left-brained, learnt side, the side of acquired knowledge, is limited to what the writer knows or has learnt.

It is useful, but because of its critical nature, a writer can often become despondent and leave the work alone. Left-brained writing can produce very clever writing, but it is mostly "thought" work, with words and language that is designed, restructured and rearranged. As a writer, you are not discovering anything new. There are no surprises and you stay much where you are, in yourself.

The left brain, then, is the place of the second hand, of thought, of things already discovered. And, in allowing the left brain to monitor and to control what the right brain brings in, one does separate the reader from the experience that is being written about. The writing then might be safe, but it is not living, fresh and original as is the writing that comes directly from the right brain.

## Chapter 6: The Right Brain

Using the right brain is writing with the imagination, where the mind sees pictures, and the senses are in full use. It takes an experience directly flashed into the mind and puts it down on paper. There is no division between the experience and the reader who is *there* where everything is happening.

This is why I like to help students build atmosphere in their imaginations and then to let it out onto their paper. Lovely, real work results.

"It's like a video in your head," I tell students, "and in your head, you use your senses. You smell things, taste them, touch them, feel them, see them, but you don't think about them. Instead, you just show us the colours, the shapes, the patterns, the light and shade, and the sounds they make." Because the rule of writing is: *show* and don't *tell*.

Tell, I say, is writing down "It was a windy day." Show, is "The wind whipped the dust into spirals and the girl bent her head." Students get the idea immediately.

The right brain has many answers to us as writers, or as teachers of writing and it is really worth understanding its whims. It is also greatly beneficial for a writer to unlock his or her creativity by getting into the right brain and then writing copiously to begin with, just anything. And then to find out ways of writing better as one proceeds along one's path as a writer, excited about all that is happening. It makes sense that, at this sensitive stage, the writer keeps the work away from the left-brained highly qualified critics.

Having generalised, let us look more carefully at this enormous sleeping partner, the right brain. It sees things in patterns. It likes complexity. It is shy, lazy and is easily hurt. It does not like criticism; this will send it into hiding and it will not come out and help. But if the right brain gets encouragement, which it needs, it will start to bring forth its treasures and when these are applauded, it will bring out more, and more and more. And as it has its connections with the past, the present and the future, the wealth that it can provide is without limit. Later, when it is strong and confident, it has a better chance of dealing with criticism.

I get my students to work creatively. I tell them that there is another way to work, the way I have just described in the previous chapter, when they deliberately choose a certain character or certain name and set action in a certain chosen place.

But I say, "Call what I do a learning experience, and go along with what I am going to ask you to do. If it works for you, you can use this afterwards. If it doesn't then just go back to what you used to do."

In almost every case, and certainly in the case of what teachers call the mixed ability group, and the attention deficit disorder students, the results are truly astonishing.

"All children in my school on medication for hyperactivity should be doing right-brained writing," said one headmistress. "It's too amazing what the unmotivated restless ones are producing. Pages and pages of written work. I can barely believe it!"

To continue with the accolade for the right brain. Where the left brain uses acquired knowledge, the right brain taps into the whole of the universe where all knowledge resides. It brings in whole plots, correct names, it works out how a story will go and ends it correctly, often in a way surprising to the author who has no idea how the story is proceeding.

I love teaching my classes and I never ask them, "What is going to happen next?" Because I know that that is death to a story.

The subconscious creative can only tell the story once, in a way that is lively, vital and interesting. If the pupil *talks* about the story before it is written, it will be boring for him to write, and flat as a pancake to listen to.

I therefore withhold my curiosity, in deference to the story my pupil is writing. Some amazing work is the result of allowing stories to shape and to tell themselves.

In fact, one writer at the workshop in Johannesburg told me that while she was writing her story, her chief character said to her, "Now please will you get up out of this chair and let me sit there. You weren't there and you don't know what was happening, but I was, so let me tell you all about it." This way your characters will definitely stay *In Character.*

Of course, it doesn't work every time. But, as Brenda Ueland says in her book, "*If You Want To Write*" if you don't like a story you've written, just leave it and write two more. Then go back and see if you like it any better. I was so glad when I read this, and thought how much better it was than saying, "Work at it until you get it right." This is often so depressing! Brenda Ueland's advice gives hope, encouragement and excitement to a writer instead of despair.

The structured school would disagree, but then I have had experience with the structured way and it is not for me. I found this out right at the beginning of my writing life when I went to a left-brained, structured school who told me how many words there should be in the first, second and third paragraphs of a story.

I remember spending the whole of a Saturday morning finding there were so many ways to write the first paragraph and all I had done was to write it over and over again, so that, after a few hours of this, I was covered in a red rash from nerves, from trying too hard to do it "right."

Fortunately I found the New Era School of Writing, in Durban, run by Fay Goldie in the 1960's. An ex Fleet Street London, journalist, an author of many books and an inspired teacher, she helped my creativity and my ideas to flow. Much of what she taught me I still use, but I have learnt a lot more since then; I have added my own special ingredients to anything I have learnt from anyone else. This has created a dynamic method that really brings results; further, I have spent a number of years studying the right brain's methods and input - and quirks.

Writing done with the right brain needs a non-judgmental and non-critical environment. In fact, a teacherless approach is what one is looking for. This means the teacher acts simply as a catalyst and if he or she says, *do this* and the student wants to *do that*, then that is fine.

The process of reading out is also done not for criticism but simply for the student to find out what he or she has written, and it is important to do this because the work is mostly far better than the writer had imagined it would be. This means a sort of "backwards" process as the right brain, first, pours out words.

Then comes a "reading out" when the person finds meaning in the writing, and finally arrives at a place and with a piece of writing, a story or even a book that would have been impossible to create with just the input of the left brain. And with a perfect title which comes *after* the writing is done. For the left brain starts out thinking it knows what it means and writes as clearly as it can after arranging paragraphs in the proper order, and correcting and changing things.

It makes sense that this is the cause of the problem of not being able to write well and easily! It means a writer is moving from the critic, your left brain, to the creative side, and back again. The critic finds another word, crosses out something. It stops to think. Writing done with the left brain is full of alterations, and it is read over silently before it is read aloud.

Now consider the right-brained approach.

The rules go like this. To begin with, you are going to write for ten minutes without stopping. You may not think before you start or write on a previously "thought about" topic. (*Thinking* is about taking control, and we are working at losing control, quite scary for the controllers in the world.)

You may not alter or change anything you write.

The helpful things are that spelling, punctuation, paragraphing and how you write is not important. To help the pencil to keep moving on the paper for ten minutes you may write the words "go, go" a couple of times or "up, up" when ideas seem to have gone. This keeps the flow of words. We also use unlined paper as this interferes as little as possible with the right-brained process of allowing first thoughts out on paper.

The right brain goes for the jugular and allows out things as the mind sees them in its first flashes and not as it thinks it ought to see them, once the internal censor comes in, which results in proper but boring work.

Doing writing in this right-brained way is based upon trust. First, it is trust for the person doing the writing, in him or herself. This trust also enlarges to include the group that person is working with. The ideal is for the writer to read out aloud what has been written; the writer is not reading out for praise or criticism.

However, because one writes for ten minutes without stopping, without altering anything, and without thinking, "scrambled eggs" can be the result. I say, that is to be expected, it is good to turn the mind upside down, and we ask for quantity and not quality. No one is getting gold stars for good work.

This is a great relief and as everyone is different, some write stories or poems, some explore words and thoughts, some start and stop and explore their minds and all of this is fine, because the mind is unscrambling itself and because when what is on top is released, then the stories will come out. Or the novel, or whatever it is you are wanting to write.

All you need is the tip of the iceberg. The rest of the sizeable mass will come out as the tip rises above the surface. It's a comforting thought, and the writers that have given me hope are the ones who have just allowed the thing to grow. In her book, *If You Want to Write,* Brenda Ueland says that, when she mentioned her book to a friend, she was asked if she had planned the book and done an outline.

She said that a coldness grew around her heart as she momentarily panicked at thought of planning such a large edifice of words. No, just start and more will come, she said. That was the advice that I am took in writing this book.

The right-brained process is about writing without knowing your meaning, and then finding meaning in your writing. Peter Elbow in his *Writing Without Teachers* says you can expect to land up some place else from where you started. He says it is about finding meaning, not about starting out with meaning.

I find it far more exciting and it does mean evolution for us as writers; we are discovering new parts of ourselves. It is deep stuff. It is soul growth. It is evolution. It is working with the noble part of oneself. And the process is different. One writes rapidly, then reads aloud. Only later does one edit the work. And one never throws away the original "unplanned" work.

You will hear people say apologetically before reading out, "I'm afraid it's a lot of rubbish." Now that is the left brain talking, the critic, and that's why it's important to read it out, because the writer will find it's not rubbish. It's a fine piece of writing, and if one does this fairly often, there will be growth in the unconscious creative, or this huge all-knowing lateral creative partner; and soon flawless right-brained writing that is of a very high standard will result. And then there is serendipity. Things turn up. Take note of them.

Your right brain knows you want to write a story or a book. It knows you believe you *can* and you are helping it with visual pictures (the goal-setting businessmen who checked their goal cards daily). Keep focussed on what you want and let your writing life be a path that keeps on and on but twists and turns as it winds its way through the interruptions that the world and life throws in the way. The right brain also brings along things that you need for your writing. They are all around you. They are signposts and your writing material. You need however to keep a quiet mind, with attention to the *now*.

## Chapter 7: Accessing Your Right Brain

*This chapter aims to unlock each person as a writer, whether from a teaching, or a writing, point-of-view.*

We are in a left-brained state, most of the time. That way, we notice the traffic lights are red, and that there is no parking in a certain zone until 8.30 am. Which, of course, is of great benefit for us in the world we live in.

It is in this left-brained way that we normally write. And that is the way that newcomers to the right-brained way of writing come to workshops and classes. I notice a newcomer to my children's classes chewing her pencil and sitting without writing.

I smile and say, "This is not school. Write anything you like. Just have fun but keep your pencil moving."

After five minutes of freewriting, following the method I am about to give you, you will sense a change. A shift. It is this shift that I mentioned in chapter two of this book, when the face loosens, the body loosens and the pencils fly, no, *dance*, along the pages. And if you keep on practising in this way, without judging yourself, you will become very accomplished and competent. In section two of this book, you will read work that students have free-written without any preplanning on their parts

The right brain is the home of music, art, religion. It is interested in complexity. And in *Drawing on The Right Side of the Brain,* Betty Edwards tells you how to move across from the left side of the brain to the right. You can actually feel the shift.

And where her way does that for artists, my way does a similar thing for writers. Only the shift is less obvious. It is more subtle.

So - know you are going to write on an unlined book with a fairly soft pencil preferably and that you are going to write to music. It is generally found that baroque music; the music of Vivaldi, Verdi, Mozart, and Haydn, will help you to keep on your creative 'high.'

There are a few things to do. Firstly are you comfortable? You will write better if you are. When I ask the children this, they often lie on the floor - they certainly move showing that the position they had been in was not really comfortable.

The next thing is to know the rules. To start with, you need to do a ten minute timed free-writing exercise: this is the ingredient with which you can do any other form of writing, be it poetry, stories, or journalism. Like cake flour, there is a lot you can do with it. We will look at ways of using right-brained creative freewriting in our approach to the traditional methods in section two.

In those ten minutes you may not stop your hand from moving on the paper at all. That means you can't stop to read it over. You can't stop to think, you can't stop to change or alter anything.

You are to lose control, as I have said before. Punctuation, spelling and other restrictions such as correct grammar go out of the window for this session.

The reason for "quantity" is that the hand must keep moving. In doing this, ideas are starting to pour in. Stop, and they disappear, and, like getting onto a bicycle again, you have to start peddling laboriously all over again. As this is a timed exercise, you cannot stop until the ten minutes is up. This allows one to transverse into sometimes dangerous or forbidden areas of the mind, and you can access some amazing information that is as vivid today as it was when it happened.

Expect surprises of all kinds when you do right-brained writing. You will become real and write real stuff.

Stuff you care about and which others will care about should you wish to share it with them. It will not be pseudo or plastic.

You may not think of a topic before you start. You may not alter anything you write. If you find you meant to say something different, just write it next to what you have been writing.

This freewriting exercise also means that you can't give your work a title because you haven't written it yet.

You may start with words, you may write a bit of poetry, you may find a story popping out, you can change mid-stream and write another idea down. Just keep going.

You may also write the words *go, go, go* (a few times only) if your mind finishes a thought and no more ideas are waiting. This gives you an idea for a bit more writing. If your ideas come to an end, you can write *up, up, up*, also just a few times as lots happens up above us. Again it can prime your pump for a bit longer.

Some people immediately go into stories. They are no better than the person who explores words and phrases, their senses and their feelings, because we each of us are dealing with our realness; we have no structures to follow and no boundaries to keep to.

Once you discover how to use this creative side of yourself, you will discover the vastness of the universe that you have accessed and with it the power and the originality that comes from being uniquely yourself.

You know the rules; now, all you need to do is to close your eyes because it is the imagination we are wanting to stimulate: keeping the eyes open binds us to the room we are in and the people who are there - it is absolutely necessary to close the eyes. Something happens when you close your eyes; somehow there is a switch from the *here and now* and *this room*, and *the people in it*, to the inner world of the imagination. In making this shift, the brain stops thinking thoughts, and allows the imagination and higher mind to bring in ideas that wouldn't have been accessed with the left brain.

Then we next do some deep in-breathing to a count of three (or four - whichever is the most comfortable) then hold the breath for a count of three, breathe out again to a count of three, hold again for three, and then repeat this three or four times. This, in scientific terms, is designed to move you from a *beta* state over to the relaxation of an *alpha* state.

Once you have established a deep easy pattern of controlled breathing, take your awareness from your breathing to your mind. I said you were not to think when you began your ten minutes writing. The only way to "not think" is simply to watch your thoughts and see what is going on in your head. This process interests the children greatly and you will not have any discipline problems with them when they are occupied in this way.

Now the movement to the creative state comes in the final stage of looking for the beginning or the end of your thoughts. You will find, strangely, there is no beginning or end, but a calm stillness instead. And the moment you get to this point, open your eyes and write the very first words that come into your mind and just keep writing, remembering you can write, *go, go*, or *up, up* but that you must not stop your pencil moving on the paper for ten minutes. It is at the start of the writing that the music quietly playing in the background should be switched on. And the idea is to enjoy oneself.

When the ten minutes is up, ask for volunteers to read out what they have written. Shy people who think they have written a lot of rubbish will be sorry that they didn't read out because, back at home they will find it a lot better than they imagined. In fact, it will be excellent.

And, by reading it out and sensing the genuine accolade in others present, the right brain is encouraged and this shy little shoot just breaking the soil of the subconscious mind is encouraged to grow a bit more.

This is your total equipment. If you say you want to write, you will be grateful to have learnt this method when there is a delayed aeroplane flight, or a shop that is opening late because of a staff training session. There will be no need to kill time. You can write - in a café, sitting on a tombstone in a graveyard, in your car, on the beach, anywhere.

This simplicity, this unleashing and unblocking of your

creativity is more important than you may realise. I have had a prospective student who insisted that she could only write on a laptop computer. She said she never wrote *anything* by hand and that she must bring it with her to my class. I didn't know how I was going to cope, especially when it came to writing with the left hand, and was relieved when the prospective student didn't arrive.

Now the computer is way ahead of the typewriter when it comes to polishing and getting a book or a story ready to go out into the world - when your left brain is in on the scene.

But to be conditioned to *having* to write initially on the computer is very restricting. This is as much a limitation to a writer as the person I heard of who had to write on orange-coloured paper, or the one who couldn't write if someone else had used her computer or sat at her chair.

The computer, for freewriting, is useful if you switch off the monitor so you can't see what you are writing. Or if you change the font to white, and then change it back to auto when you have done your writing for that session. In these ways, you will keep the left brain's interference out of the new work you are creating.

Also very useful to read is the book *Becoming a Writer* by Dorothea Brande which is one that every writer should study. In this book, Dorothea Brande prescribes two books to write in daily. One is an early morning freewriting book that you use as you open your eyes and write in for five to ten minutes.

Please note that this book is not for other people to read. Your subconscious would not let out truths about you if it thought it was for appraisal by others. You also shouldn't read it yourself for two weeks as you do not want associative writing. In other words, each day what you write must be just what is happening in your mind as you wake up.

This means you don't get a cup of tea or wake up properly - you are to remain trance-like, so that you are surprised at what you read in your book because you do not even remember writing it. You will get inner knowledge of yourself - and you may find that what you thought interested you most as a writer, is quite different from what you, the real person, would like to write about.

This early morning freewriting has more benefits than this. It geometrically increases the output of any other writing you are doing during the day. It gets you writing if you have stopped and don't know how to get started again.

It also gives you your voice and your power as a writer. This is your effect on others, the way you move them to laughter or to tears, or to changing things for themselves. The ability to do this will mark you as a writer. (Peter Elbow likens writing to catching a snake in order to put it in a bottle. If you kill it, it is of no use. You need to catch it alive.)

Further, the mind is slippery and elusive. It's your mind and you often think you know yourself. But writing gives you a good chance to see if you really do.

You have a comfort zone. The right brain likes you the way you are. If you decide you want to write, not only do you need to do early morning freewriting for five to ten minutes daily, but you need a second book in which you write, on time, at any time chosen by yourself, for another ten minutes daily. This could be the freewriting session described in this chapter.

For the first three days after learning about these two books that you are to write in for a mere twenty minutes daily, you will find no trouble in doing this. But watch yourself for excuses after the third day.

Your right brain may think, "This looks like trouble. Why should we change?" And because the right brain is lazy, as well as unwieldy, for three days it will let you do as you say you are going to do. Then on the fourth day, challenge your excuses as to why you can't write for five or ten minutes when you first wake up, or you can't find ten minutes in the day to write on time. Write your way through your excuses and see what your mind is thinking up for you so as to avoid the tedium of the writing. It is most interesting, and I once had a writer who just wrote through an urge to get up and defrost the fridge and another urge to empty the post box. These, and other things of a similar nature, would have meant the end of the ten minutes freewriting, and probably her interest in being a writer.

In fact, Dorothea Brande goes so far as to say that if you can't meet with yourself on time each day, don't think of writing as a career for yourself, but go and find something else creative. To be a good writer, you must learn to meet with yourself daily, when both your conscious and subconscious minds can come together: in this way you will learn to write elegantly and well. Your subconscious will give up objecting, and gracefully play the part you require it to play, that of bringing along the wonderful ideas and creativity that will enrich your writing.

And as an observer of many thousands of people as they write, I will tell you there is a wonderful sense of joy and harmony that children or adults have as they write creatively. Music keeps this "high".

All this is healthy too. Relaxation and enjoyment are keys to good health. Stress and anxiety make all kinds of negative changes occur in the body. This right-brained way of writing relaxes the body and turns the hard work of creative writing into something that is fun and full of surprising imaginative bits.

All this builds self-esteem and better health, it is therapeutic because it brings to the surface hurts and worries that are often long buried. Once made conscious, they can be looked at, and then let go. One of the teachers at a workshop I gave for the Association for Professional Educators of KwaZulu Natal said a student at her high school thanked her for teaching her this freewriting because she had had a tangle of problems and by freewriting she had sorted them out.

It is a good idea to read Dorothea Brande's *Becoming A Writer* where she gives the function of the left brain, to protect the right brain from harsh criticism before it is ready to deal with it.

That is why I advise students to read their writing out to their cat or a favourite plant. One student read it out to her bird who was very encouraging and nodded its head.

This is also why I will only give workshops to children in schools after their teachers have had a workshop. It would be too easy for the teacher to totally destroy the new ability of the child which is still coming out in cumbersome form if the teacher hadn't personally experienced the delight of work coming from the right brain.

It is also very destructive to harshly criticise people who read out their freewriting. This is another reason that workshops should only be run in an atmosphere that is truly non-judgmental and non-critical. Because the only reason for reading aloud is for the person to find out what he or she has written; to find out that the great sleeping right brained partner has truly helped language to be used in a better way and that this writing from the heart and the feelings captures one's own interest along with genuine reader interest. It is this true knowing of our greatness that helps to grow a writer's belief that he or she *can* write - if there is a real desire.

I often have queries from students about the value of writing on the computer compared with writing by hand. I have read somewhere that writing emotional scenes by hand is best. It is quite all right to move over to your computer when you find an idea and the words are coming too fast, and anyway, for action writing, the computer is fine.

Now that I've given you some background to the pro's and con's of free-writing by hand and by computer, let us focus on the task ahead which is going right-brained and just writing, then taking our work and finding a market for it. As I said, everything works very efficiently - backwards!

# PART TWO: USING THE CREATIVE PROCESS

## CHAPTER 8: INTRODUCTION TO PART TWO

Within many people there is the urge to write. For the vast majority this will be just an unfulfilled wish - something they would have *liked* to do. But for the few who have found the secret that unlocks this creativity, they will know the true joy of a writer who is able to live two exciting lives at one and the same time.

This book shows - it helps - perhaps it will become the tool to unlock those who have felt that they *can't* write. For there are many kinds of people who want to write. Ages of people I have taught vary from five years to eighty five. The form of the writing content is as varied as their ages. Some would like to do journalism, some short stories, some biographies, some poetry.

I run courses that work for many different kinds of people. Sometimes one person comes alone. A student in grade 11 who couldn't write *anything* in his English essay lesson, was sent to me by his private school. He learnt freewriting, and then fiction techniques. He wrote non stop for the period of one hour that he was with me. His work was of a high standard.

I said, "Did you enjoy this?"

He said, "It was all right."

I said, "You can write, you know that, don't you?"

He inclined his head.

"The answer to your problem is in your hands. If you choose to, you can. Come back if you need help."

He never did and I checked with his private school to see how he was doing. He had passed his English exam by the skin of his teeth and, the teacher said, it was only because of his good marks in the essay section.

A woman who thought she couldn't get words down on paper but wanted to write articles found writing was easy. A lawyer who couldn't write legal letters discovered they were no problem. An astronomer whose book had stuck found a new direction and finished the book in a month. A woman who didn't expect to write anything at a novel workshop, found the start of a novel and had finished it after three months.

A German whose book in German had come to a halt unblocked and she ripped away, reading out, in German, what she had written, of which I could understand not a word. But she was so happy!

A school where the Zulu students didn't write in Zulu any longer invited me along for an hour. The children wrote poetry and stories and laughed in delight at each other's work - all written in Zulu. (Again, I didn't know the language.) In every one of these cases, the method worked. But I must admit that I didn't know it was going to be *that* successful, as I sat with my feet in the swimming pool, seven years ago, and devised a writing course that was different. That would help people to write. And finally, me, to write this book.

I had been writing for many years before I decided to teach. During this time, I had been on so many courses that had inspired me to rush home and to write. But I remember so well that on the first day, I would find that, by the end of it, I had done no writing at all. Deciding that it was now too late and I was tired, I would promise myself that I would write the next day. The same thing happened, with me feeling guiltier and guiltier about not doing what I professed I so badly wanted to do. To write. And then the deadline energy that came along suddenly had the story or article done, just in time, on the morning of the next lecture, one week later.

That wasn't going to be so with the course *I* would give. It would accommodate everyone's needs. If they didn't know why they wanted to write, they would write and find out. One woman recently found poetry pouring from her. If a person wanted to write a novel but didn't know how to do so, we'd find out. And we did. By relaxation exercises, imagination stretching exercises, and fantasy exercises. All of these were right-brained. And then, unexpectedly, the book would announce itself. Its shape would be there.

If a person wanted to write children's work, then we'd study the world's good children's writers to see what it was that made them published and popular. They'd find their unique 'self' and write good original and exciting children's stories *their* way. And it worked too.

To maintain success however is the real test. This means adapting to the needs of people and of publishers, of studying current trends in people's reading choices.

This is the tedious part called 'market research' and though my approach is back-to-front, and mildly arrogant, at some time it is necessary to find the shape your creation is to take and the angle to which you need to slant it along with, possibly, the number of words. It is this disciplined approach (call it *whole-brained*) that will make you successful. You will find much of this information in the chapters that follow.

The answer lies in your gigantic creative partner, the right brain, the home of creativity of all kinds. Some people never fitted into the school system, and this has conditioned them to feel they are not okay. And some who fitted the school system might have been creative people but their focus changed at school. Some know this, and are able to make the change from left-brained occupations to right-brained ones, which brings them happiness and fulfilment.

Somewhere I read that life is lived forwards and understood backwards. I understand that what I am doing now can only be the result of living my life exactly as I have done - though many times I have questioned - why? Why am I doing this particular thing?

I say this because all of what I am currently doing, (from the teaching of many different children and adults in many different kinds of situation, to the publishing of many kinds of books written by my talented students,) could only have happened because of my life's experiences in writing, art, photography, teaching, editorship - and accounting. It helps, too, that I have discovered my right brain.

Many clever hardworking people are unaware of their creative partner. One secretary wrote me a wonderful letter after a course. She had some poetry published in an in-house magazine of a business that she worked for, and she was amazed to find there were hundreds of answers to problems, hundreds of choices, when before she had thought there was only one route and one choice. The one her left brain gave her.

This right-brained writing changes people, for the good. One student said at a recent workshop, “Something in me changed this weekend. I am a different person.”

She said it with a shine in her eyes and with confidence in her voice.

## Chapter 9: So You Want To Write A Better Letter?

Creative freewriting can produce a really interesting letter.

I once had a woman come to me for a month's course of lessons because her daughter now lived overseas and she was losing touch with her. She knew the letters she was writing were being written and rewritten, and polished and edited until they were flat and boring. It was important to her that her letters were good as her daughter had married a man with a title.

Creative freewriting for ten minutes without stopping was a terribly hard thing for her to do. In her years at school she had been trained to write a letter "properly", and now, asking her to lose control, was like asking her to swim the length of the pool underwater without coming up for breath. She told me that.

But she persisted and after a month of lessons, she was writing poetry and freewriting on unlined onion skin paper the most interesting and lively letters. I have one myself because she thanked me with a five-page letter written non stop without thinking. That, for her, was the ultimate success where writing was concerned.

Challenges that come my way are many and varied. One Saturday morning brought me a young lawyer who was having trouble writing legal letters.

Lawyers, accountants and architects are amongst the people who find it hardest to become right-brained. Their trained, very clever left brains are often unaware of their right brain partners. I told this lawyer a bit about it.

"I'll teach you freewriting and then creative ways of writing your letters," I said. "Everything is backwards to what you ever learnt. You find meaning from writing. You don't write knowing your meaning." I explained the process.

"It sounds bizarre," said my left-brained legal student.

This was gong to be difficult, especially as the man's wife

had sent him. However, with work piled all around him he was desperate enough to believe I could help him.

I continued. "You need to know the left brain is arrogant. It is opinionated. It's a know-all and it meddles. You cross out and change because of the left brain. Of course you need a whole brain but before that you need to storm into the right brain to get its riches. To do that you need the left brain to take a lunch break. So I'm going to tell you the rules which are simply, write for ten minutes without stopping. Don't think before you start, and you can't cross out or change anything you write." He understood all of this.

I gave him the rules. He wrote for ten minutes in beautiful stylish language but with real feeling. I told him about early morning free-writing, adding, "And you'll find a whole lot about yourself you didn't know."

I had given him the lists to do, both in his right hand and left hand which may have shown him that he had been keeping secrets from himself.

"If you allow yourself to accept the help from your subconscious, you'll find unexpected things coming to you." I mentioned that in M. Scott Peck's book *The Road Less Travelled* the word "Pinocchio" kept on coming into his mind when he was consulting with a patient who had a problem. Then he realised - puppet - this woman was a puppet who was just acting out a part but had no real life. He had his answer!

"So once you learn to freewrite, which will get problems off the top of your head, you'll find yourself free to notice when your subconscious pops things into your head to help with problems you have. This is usually when it's inconvenient, you're in the shower, driving the car, playing golf, whatever, but you need to jot one word down which will bring the whole thought back to you.

"Notice again, the left brain is momentarily not in control and your silent partner has a chance to slip in an answer for you."

We had a lot of time left and I asked my student if he knew about branching or mind mapping. I find this amazingly useful. I can write chapters or speeches or even books and novels, and I explained.

"You have this legal letter to write. Let's "branch" it. Put the topic in the centre, then mind map it by rapidly drawing spider legs out from the centre and then on each leg put the points as they come to you. You can draw more legs off each leg with sub-points. It gives you a chance to get in more information and to go further than if you wrote lists. And it keeps the points all in logical order."

The young lawyer did this.

"Now just dictate your letter, using this branched diagram," I said.

He did a perfectly good legal letter with all the details and information necessary, in a minute or two.

"You see how easy it is," I said. "You'll have loads more time and loads less stress."

We talked about research and how he felt one could research too much and not know where to start. Or what to use. I told him a right-brained way of writing a letter when you haven't done the research but you write it anyway, glossing over the details of the research, but at the same time unearthing the research that you need to do to complete this task. I told him he would be pleased to find the exact research that he would need to do with no waste of time and energy in finding out things that he didn't need to know.

**Writing letters to magazines**

Read a magazine, find some article you agree or disagree with, and then you will have a topic for a letter which the magazine could like. Now close your eyes, either do some breathing or take one long deep conditioning breath which tells you that you are going right-brained. Look at your thoughts and when they slow down momentarily put the article into your mind's eye. Then without stopping to think, open your eyes and write a letter. When you have finished, read it aloud, and then you will need to go through it to keep the writing lean. This means, to remove superfluous words. But don't spoil the first fresh way of writing it

Writing letters to magazines or newspapers fine-tunes your mind to crisp writing. It also gets your name known to readers and editors. And it is a way to easily be published; this is your first step to believing you can have a career as a writer. Many magazines pay you for writing letters that they can publish.

## Chapter 10: Whoever heard of Creative Journalism?

For eighteen months I gave weekly lectures in various writing genre at the Bartels Art Trust Centre on the yacht mole in Durban. This was a splendid venue for creative writing, with the pink clouds of the setting sun reflecting over the mirrored waters of the bay and the gulls wheeling overhead.

Journalism was popular and at one course Clayton Montgomery, a young man with a band called Halcyon, came to learn to write.

"In Johannesburg, they had the information about the bands in Durban all wrong. I phoned to tell them and they asked if I could write. I said I could and so they asked me to write a column," he said. "But I've never written a thing before."

"Not to worry, we'll make your statement true," I said.

In doing the ten minute session on creative writing, he and other journalists often wrote material that could be shaped into letters which a few of them had published in the Saturday paper and other magazines. Other freewriting could be used for creatively written articles.

This way of writing means that the material is gathered first, from the freewriting, and then the journalist needs to shape it to fit a suitable market. This actually makes writing a lot easier as your topic is written, and what you write, in some way, directs the market you'll need to find.

With Clayton, all went well. Using the creative method of rapidly freewriting, then reading it over and freewriting it again, he came up with an interesting article that he finally shaped correctly. His first published article on the Party Train and the annual band competition at Splashy Fen in Natal was eloquently written and he was proud of it.

Clayton now writes a Friday morning column for a Durban newspaper reviewing live music venues and live bands; and he compiles a basic weekly gig guide.

Freewriting can be used in articles for dozens of magazines, newspapers, and journals.

For instance, you may have freewritten about something thrown up from your subconscious that was funny, hair-raising, or tragic. You will find the writing is good, and what you need to do is to target it at the right market. "It happened to me," "My story," and "Last page" are some of the slots that magazines have available for the freelancer.

There are other specialist magazines, like car magazines and in-house magazines, to which you can also tailor an article. You will find that an article on birds can be used in a motoring magazine if you include the car and the journey as well.

Once you have got the idea, you will find countless slots for articles jumping up at you, and countless pieces of material for you to write on.

You will need to do certain things in addition.

Your finished article needs to be professional

Newspaper journalism requires that the five W's be dealt with in the first paragraph. These are *who, why, when, where,* and *what.*

But today even newspaper journalism is changing. People are getting used to reading the first paragraph and skipping the rest of the article as they know the outcome. So, to get readers involved in the whole article, publications often resort to the fiction technique of story telling, where the final exciting fact is kept to the last paragraph. Writers need to study magazine and newspaper articles for themselves to see how topics are handled, and which methods they find the best, and also what are the preferences of the publications to which they wish to submit articles.

Other important information you need when writing an article is: title, length, the look of the article on paper (variety of sentences, beginnings to paragraphs, with the use of dialogue to make it look interesting), how it sounds as you read it aloud. You also need lean writing, an intriguing beginning, a neat end, and a catchy title.

Type your article in double-line spacing and print it out with good black ink. You need a cover sheet which gives your name and address in the top right hand corner, the title of the article (keep it to five words if possible) and your name or non de plume in the centre.

In the bottom right hand corner, type in the number of words, the fact that it is an article, the number of illustrations (if any) and state "First South African Serial Rights" if you are offering it for sale in South Africa. Note that you may not send it to more than one magazine or newspaper in one country at the same time. You may also offer to sell the same article in another country, in which case you offer, for instance, "First Australian Serial rights." Note that you are not selling your copyright. You are selling the use of it only.

Travel is a specialised topic which needs an anecdotal or personal touch to bring it to life. If you write humour, which is always popular, please note that it is best written "dead pan" just in case the reader's sense of humour differs from your own. This way, you never come off looking stupid - and you can win by being very funny which is your real aim.

You now have to apply the rules of marketing which are: Who will read the magazine and your article? What sort of article does the magazine publish? How long are their articles? Are they written by freelancers or editorial staff?

Answers to all the above questions come by checking the advertising, checking the readers' letters, and checking the editorial to gauge who reads the magazine and what the editor wants.

You find out which articles they pay for by finding the freelance slots; if you check the names of the editorial staff in the front of the magazine, you can know that, if any of the articles are written by any of these people, they are staff reporters, and that this is part of their job. So this slot is not available for freelancers.

Now to put the final polish to your freewriting.

Check that you do have a catchy title of not more than

five words, a 'hook' beginning that draws the reader into the article, and an ending that ties up with the beginning and the title to make it all feel "right."

Here follows extracts from an article published in one of our major magazines; it was illustrated colourfully and humorously. This article which started life as a free-writing exercise, was timed to tie in with the marathon the following year.

Peggy Harper's article, "*I Ran It My Way*," is humour at its best. With her permission, here are four excerpts - the article was published in Personality Magazine on 19th May 1995.

**I RAN IT MY WAY**

I should have been in bed with my husband, the Sunday paper and a try of tea and hot, buttered toast, I thought, as I gazed around, eyes like a magpie's. Fancy being in a race. Whatever had possessed me? There I was, awash in a sea of Lycra at 8 am on a Sunday morning in my blindingly new takkies. A seething mass of nubile young things, keen as mustard, stretched away in front of me and disappeared into the distance behind me.

There was also a smattering of women like myself - old enough to know better.

*********

The noise was reaching a crescendo. Four thousand hyped-up women, off the leash for an hour or two with no male to say, "Tone it down there a little, Susie." Heady stuff.

Shrieks of girlish laughed rippled periodically through the crowd as the inevitable pantomime dames pranced through on obscenely hairy legs, frilly pink tutus barely covering their Y fronts, balloon bosoms straining at the monstrously huge, white bras.

We stood and sweltered, waiting for the start... I toyed with the idea of slinking away before I disgraced myself by failing to finish this 10-kay walking race. How long was 10-kays, anyway?

"Forget it, " the others laughed, "you'll never get your car out of the parking area, it's chock-a-block."

Well, that was that, then.

Then came a muffled sound like a gunshot away up front and, unless it was a balloon breast exploding, it must have been the starter's gun. We were packed in too closely to move forward and the seconds ticked by.

Slowly that gigantic female shongololo got underway with its 8 000 designer takkies, each pair the equivalent value of Uganda's GNP, shuffling forward. And so did I, in my Hyperbola specials, made somewhere east of Taiwan.

*********

Then I made a bad error. I turned around.

This is obviously the runner's equivalent of a climber clinging to a rock face and taking a quick look down. The horrible realisation dawned - I was all but last. Only two or three of the most hopeless were flopping and lolloping along behind me. And behind them was the ambulance, cruising patiently like a vulture stalking its dying prey. Through the windscreen I caught a glimpse of cool, unsmiling male faces, the sun glinting off Ray Bans ...

*********

Just as we began eyeing the bushes speculatively, we rounded a corner and there ahead lay glorious beachfront loos. And showers. The din of bellowing testosterone-laden voices raised in lusty song resounded from the Men/Amadodo section, where macho men fresh from the surf were showering.

Relieved and ready to race, I tore out again a few minutes later. I'd have to really move now to make up for precious time lost. At that moment raucous laughter brayed from the showers and a flasher, flourishing his family jewels, leapt out and struck a pose before me.

I was incensed. How dare he ruin my time! Almost bowling him over, I thundered past, shouting, "Put it away, there's a good fellow. This is a race, you know."

The silence from the Men/Amadodo block was deafening. We were convulsed.

*********

Magazines are businesses that have to make a profit, have to bring in new readers and not lose current ones. This means you need to exactly study the mind-set of the magazine. You can do this by getting a year's supply of magazines and reading every article for the freelancers' slots, one after the other. You can call this 'work' if you are seriously interested in writing articles for magazines. You then enter your findings into a magazine market study book with columns for author, title, word number, type of writing, subject matter, angle, beginning, ending and so on.

But whether you do this or not, after reading a consecutive lot of articles from one magazine you will be in the magazine editorial staff's mind-set and right at this moment it is a good time to write an article of your own that would fit their requirements and those of their readers. Just think of an article they haven't got in that magazine that could easily be in it if there was space for it, and you could find that what you write will fit - and sell to them.

It's no good deciding that a practical magazine for people without gardens should have something about flowers to make them like flowers. That isn't going to work and you'll just be rejected. And dejected. If you did a thoughtless thing like this, it might be time to again ask the question. Do you really want to write? Because if you do, you'll do what works best to make it a success for you.

## Chapter 11: Writing Short Stories

Definitions of the short story are many and a creative approach could be that trouble is landing, has landed, or is about to land as the story starts.

You could say, also, that a short story is about solving a relationship or making a decision. It is about strong feelings, and the problem must matter desperately to the chief character. A short story is about change. Things are not the same; the chief character is not the same at the end of the story.

There is a pattern to a short story. A short story is also told from one viewpoint, creates one emotion in the reader's mind and is about one thing that is happening. It is lean and sleek, and goes in a straight line, with no extraneous characters or happenings. It is complete in its wholeness and somehow the beginning and the end tie up.

A short story starts in a tense situation and things get progressively worse as the person takes action. Note that it is because of this action that the problem gets solved, not because some outside force or person provided the solution.

The elements in a short story are the character with a strong emotional problem, the background and the atmosphere, dialogue and the plot (the way the story moves from beginning to end.)

You can write a story in different ways. You may get an idea for an ending, and then you have to think of the beginning. You may get an idea for a story and then you need to find the characters that would suit this, and where the story could take place. Or you might like to write a story in a totally creative way, where you let either the atmosphere arrive in your mind, and then the character with his or her problem. Or the character first, with the background he or she is in.

Let us start with atmosphere, or setting.

In this case, use the method of getting creative and moving

over to your creative side before writing. Do this by closing your eyes, doing some deep breathing, and then looking at your thoughts. When you mind is still, wait for a place to come into your head. Now use your senses of touch, taste, feel, smell and sound. These are not only *words*, but if you really experience them yourself, they will take your reader right into the story which will have an evocative feeling to it. Remember there is weather, seasons, time of year, and you need to get the feel of this in your story as well as where the setting might be: in the country, a forest, a town, a church, a harbour, a high rise building or on a yacht on the bay. Or anywhere at all.

Know that when you are working with your creative unconscious, there is no right or wrong way. Whatever way your story develops, is the right way. Get right into it. See the grass and the sand, notice the paint on the walls, and the sunshine and shadows. See the clothes that people are wearing, feel the atmosphere that prevails. Look at the sky and see if there are clouds. Your story will find its way into your mind if you will just keep watching your thoughts until your mind is still. Once your story person arrives, wait, with your eyes closed. Then zoom in from a distance to some small detail.

And then you can mentally say to your character, "What's the problem?" Then as soon as your character moves or speaks, just open your eyes, pick up your pen and start writing, and just keep writing.

A video will unfold in your mind and all you need to do is to watch the video and to let the pictures you are seeing and the words you are hearing come off your pencil onto your paper.

Your story will tell itself, and even find a conclusion that you would never have expected.

Also know that you must never manipulate your characters by trying to make the story go a certain way. You must let your characters direct the story, and if for any reason you get stuck, know you're going down a wrong path. Then just back track a bit, and shut your eyes, take a deep breath, watch your thoughts, see the story at the point where it was working, and as it starts to move again, open your eyes and write!

Here is a story by Brian Duckitt, Chairman of the South African Writers' Circle and Competitions Manager who attended a one day workshop at umSinsi House in 1998. This story was published the same year in umSinsi Press' Volume 4 of *South African Short Stories* called *Voices*. The story is called *Clever Umlungu*

## CLEVER UMLUNGU

Somebody once described a microlight as a beach umbrella being chased by an angry lawnmower. Shortly after they started flying in the States, I chanced upon a two-page spread in American aviation magazine. What I saw was an incredible, multi-coloured, magic carpet. The wings were of bright fabric. They billowed gracefully, were not rigid and metallic, but soft and delicate...a giant butterfly...brilliant. The pilot sat right out in the open, the wind blowing in his face. He looked utterly free. I was hooked.

Having completed an instructor's course in Albuquerque, New Mexico, I brought one back from the States, neatly folded, as excess baggage, in the hold of a 707.

Customs asked me what it was. Truthfully, I declared that it was an aircraft. The official looked distinctly unsettled. He waved me through without further ado.

"Obviously deranged," he whispered to his assistant, nodding in my direction.

My first customer was an intense little man. He had been a light plane pilot for many years, and knew all there was to know about flying. People like that make difficult pupils.

Flying a microlight is different to anything else. All aircraft do have one thing in common. If you do not treat them with respect, they kill you. There are old pilots, and there are bold pilots...no old, bold, pilots.

Those early models had small engines. They were strictly single seaters. Students were taught to fly like young birds, running progressively faster along the ground without taking off, until they got the 'feel' of the controls.

Thereafter, under the watchful eye of instructor, they would make little hops, going a bit higher, a bit further every time. If he saw a problem, the instructor would discuss it with the pupil and demonstrate the correct technique.

When judged competent the pupil would be sent on his first circuit of the field, but only in calm, or very light wind conditions.

That's the way it's supposed to go, but some students know better...

It was late in the afternoon. The wind was picking up. Although he was almost ready to 'solo', weather conditions were not right; it was too windy. My student would have to wait until morning.

An expectant audience of friends and relatives looked distinctly disappointed. They had become bored with all the trundling up and down; wanted some action. It was bad luck. Come back tomorrow.

I was tying my microlight down behind a hanger, when an agitated crowd surrounded me. Everybody shouted. Many pointed downwind, towards the darkening horizon.

Restoring some sort of order, I discovered that my pupil, impatient with the careful training programme, and perhaps trying to impress the audience, had taken off without permission.

Being very light, with the stature of a jockey, the strong wind just carried him away. He had regained the group's attention and concern.

I was persuaded, rather reluctantly, to go and look for him, to find out if he had made a deep, possibly painful, impression elsewhere: on mother earth for instance.

Flying into the gathering gloom, being bounced about in turbulent conditions, was **not** going to be fun.

The alternative of losing and then abandoning my first pupil, was equally unattractive. It was sure to make the headlines and discourage prospective students, so ruining my business.

I found him in the new graveyard, on the outskirts of town. Nice and quiet. Not a permanent resident, you understand, just sitting on a stone, meditating. He had set down on a grassy walkway, between the disinterested occupants of the place. He was all in one piece. Any landing you can walk away from is a good one.

The flight back was a turbulent nightmare, fighting a howling gale. It was black as pitch by the time I made it back over the field. The ground was one great black hole... dark as Hades.

More by good luck than anything else, I made a safe landing, feeling my way down until I heard the wheels touch the grass. Rolling to a stop, I was surrounded by the mob-like Lindbergh in Paris. Relieved by my encouraging news, the 'friends and relatives' drove off in column, hooting and cheering, to collect their hero.

In most places cavalcades to the cemetery are much quieter affairs.

Parked once more behind the hanger, out of the wind, I sat in the machine, waiting for my heart to slow down. An airport security guard appeared out of the gloom.

He looked at me, smiled.

"Oouw. Umlungu very clever." I basked in his admiration.

"It was nothing, really. All part of the job." I waved airily.

The guard studied the aluminium tubes and steel cables which held the microlight together.

He looked at me with disbelief and concern.

"Umlungu also mad!"

Turning away, shaking his head, he delivered his final judgement.

"Umlungu more mad than clever."

*** (Published by umSinsi Press in *South African Short Stories Volume 4, Voices*, in 1998 ISBN 1-919721-78-9)

Writing magazine stories is highly courted. For some reason, it seems to be a main attraction for some writers. This writing for magazines is highly competitive and you absolutely must know exactly the story that each magazine (or the one that you are wanting to be published in) is wanting.

To start learning what ingredient it is that makes a story saleable, you need to read each story *twice*, once to get your general idea of pleasure, surprise, and enjoyment. The second reading of the same story is much more analytical. You see who is the main character, that it is written from one point of view, what is the insoluble deep emotional problem, who is the protagonist, what happens, and how the story ends, if it is solved happily or not. You see how setting and character are woven together, you note contrasts and conflicts. You are not going to copy the story, but you need to learn the ingredients of successful magazine writing.

Also consider the odds. Magazines come out monthly. That means they need twelve or perhaps twenty-four stories per annum. Many run annual competitions for winning stories. Why? Because they are collecting the next year's stories so the magazine can keep up its excellent reputation for fiction.

As in the case of writing articles, it is necessary to remember that magazines are businesses.

You do exactly the same for market study for short stories as you do when studying the feature and article market. Get a year's supply of the magazine whose stories you like best. As for the chapter on journalism, rule columns for author, title, words, names, plot, setting, type of writing, beginning, ending and so on. And the title is so important.

In just the same way as you might have done with articles, once you've read a consecutive lot of stories you will be again in that magazine editorial staff's mind-set and right now you could write that story that they might want to buy. Remember that it must be professional in every way. It must read well, sound good, look good, and fit the market.

## Chapter 12: How Do You Write A Book?

I chuckled when I read somewhere that a famous novelist writes her book and when it's finished, she prays to God for a plot and then goes to bed. I chuckled yet again when I heard that same novelist dictates six thousand words a day with her secretary seated behind her, where she can't be seen.

From these two small examples I would like you to understand that there are as many ways of writing novels as there are of people and that anything I can say here is only of general value.

To start with, might I mention that there are two main groups of books.

There is the pattern book with its gigantic prepared market that fits into a specialised series brought out by a publisher. A pattern book can pay a writer very well with the royalties on the sales of thousands of books perhaps translated into many languages.

Then there is the creative novel which, while it is much more interesting to write because it will have a unique flavour, is also very difficult to place. This is because the author will need to find a publisher who is prepared to take the risk of publishing, promoting and investing time and money in the book to make it a success.

Writing a book in the patterned way takes a lot of guesswork out of it, and gives to a degree a focused, directly-in-front of you way to write. A much published author of romantic novels took an idea I had and while I was making lunch, she wrote my first three chapters in simple phrases, much like a one-line continuity script for television, that took the action forwards. She gave me an easy way of writing. Eighteen hand-written pages with two hundred and fifty words to the page make one chapter of four thousand five hundred words; ten of these (with three scenes to a chapter) give you a ten-chapter book of forty-five thousand words.

Talking to her, I discovered that you don't actually need *anything* to write stories and be a professional author. She belonged to a Romantic Author's Society in the United Kingdom. She had written twenty three published books when I met her.

She had no computer, owned no car nor property but travelled a lot around the world seeing her children in different countries - and she wrote by hand. When she was finished, she then gave the manuscript to her typist. In Durban I entertained her for lunch. She was to speak to the Writers' Circle here.

For reasons of differentiation let us say that pattern writing means an original story, with a character that readers care for and a story that fascinates, is not predictable and is told through the eyes of the main character. And it fits into the writing scheme of publishers who run various series.

However, an exact knowledge of their various requirements and what they are publishing is vital. Most of the big publishers have marketing departments who are very willing to send information on their requirements. Some years back, Mills and Boon sent me, on request, a lot of information on the various series that they publish. There was their gentle "love" or "Rose" series and their "Desire series"; and they also had various other series.

Even with this information there is more you need to do before you begin writing your book. You need to find writers who have been published in the series that interests you. If you find an author with twenty or thirty published books this person obviously knows his or her craft and is 'read' or the publisher would not have taken on all these books.

Now check the date of publication of the book that author wrote the very first time. Then check to see what the current book is like. This gives you encouragement because you can know that the author has grown in the past ten years to where she or he currently is.

Keep abreast of current thinking. The new millennium,

women's ability to make choices where the home and job market is concerned, AIDS, all come in to your character development and your writing. The Artists' and Writers' Year Book can be a great help in finding agents to market your book for you.

Now, for those of you who long to write a book and don't mind not earning that R100000 in royalties from the "series" books, but just want to get your ideas and your experiences down into the form of a book, I'll list seven different ways you could write your book. You will, however, need to find the right editor, and literary agent to help you: this book just shows you how to tap into the creativity of the right brain to do your initial raw writing. This may make the process seem cumbersome and inefficient, but in the long run you'll get a better book and it's not really so hard to clean it up and get it "right".

Think of the book as being done in two sections.

The first, the hardest, is finding your book and your characters and getting it down without doing any reading back, changing or editing as you write. The second part is getting it right. Sorting it out. Cleaning it up. Refining it. Cutting out irrelevancies. Reading it aloud. This may seem difficult but actually it is not too bad.

If you know your subject and research carefully what you don't know, if you write with passion and keep your viewpoint to preferably one main character, you can end up with a saleable and very original novel.

Remember, write what you want to write, and not what you think others would like to buy. Remember, too, that a book has a life of its own and there is such a thing as the evolution of a novel. In other words, it doesn't come out in the exact shape you designed it.

When the story comes alive it may direct itself in a better direction.

Here are seven ways of writing a creative novel, all of which I have used.

These are:

1. Just start freewriting. You can either start with a quiet mind and let a character with a strong emotional problem in an interesting setting come into your mind, and then follow him or her as the actions take place.

Note, the operative word is *passion*. If you are not emotionally involved, or if you are cold or clinical in your writing, you're not likely to grab people and keep them glued to your writing, eagerly wondering what is going to happen next.

2. Loop or out-to-sea-writing - this method was explained to me in one of my mentors, Peter Elbow's, book, *Writing With Power*. In this method, perhaps altered slightly by my interpretation, you free write for ten or twenty minutes, then read over what you have written, and precis the whole thing in not more than half a dozen words.

Put these words in a block in the centre of the page and then using this as the starting point, get your mind quiet, and again freewrite - the direction of the story will move at a tangent. Keep doing this and then direct your idea back to the beginning. I have got two huge volumes of a fascinating story that was the result of using this method. I can recommend it for finding your story in an unusual way.

3. Create a file with twelve section divisions. Just work in each section as necessary and grab ideas as they pass you by and you have an excellent semi-controlled method where all your material is kept together between the two covers of a file. Somehow, it feels as if you really *are* writing a book.

The twelve sections are: **title, plotting** (or how to discover your story outline,) **situation** (or what was happening when the story began), **problem** (just brainstorm yourself for all the good and bad things that could happen), **characters.** (These will develop as you write; know their ages, psychological makeup, relationship, characters and what they look like.) Once you have an idea of your story you can break it up into **chapters.** Another section is **background,** then there is

**research, check, inserts, brilliant words** that sparkle, and the last one is the **nursery** (where the germ of a new book is incubating and which has the same section divisions but in mini-form.)

4. Phyllis Whitney in her *Guide to Fiction Writing* gives precise instructions on a method that I approve of. It is a combination of the 'file' mentioned above, but has in addition a way of growing extra material by free writing on both character and plot, moving from one to the other as more material surfaces. She believes in writing what you *know*, and using your own backyard as the background. This gives believability.

She also says that you need just the glimmering of an idea, and you work from here to build your material and then your book. This means that you may have just an inkling of what the chief character is worried about, and from that you free-write and when some action or plotting occurs, you turn to the section on plotting. Here you free write a whole lot more and you will find the protagonist and more of your story elements appearing.

When characters appear, again you move back to your section on characters, start a new page for this next character, and just explore him or her. Continue in this way, plotting and exploring character. If you do this for several weeks you will find there is enough material to write a short outline. You then make a circle, and divide it into segments. Each of these is a chapter. Now put perhaps three brief incidents in each chapter. This circle with its segments (or chapters) is your right-brained book and you can write the book from this, very easily.

5. You may "branch" the book. This works very well. This is mind-mapping and this is also excellent for the information book. Here you simply put your main idea in the centre of a page, and then make spider legs out, with ideas coming out fast as you do this. You can also make a series of these mind maps, one for each chapter. It is a very quick and effective

way of giving birth to the shape of a book, and knowing exactly how to tackle it without taking away the excitement of writing it by doing too much plotting.

6. You may simply get an idea, a character, a beginning and an ending and decide before writing how you are going to get from the beginning to the end. My book, *The Wild Swarm*, was begun in this way, but a short way along the path it stuck and wouldn't continue. Writers' block had descended upon me. I stopped writing the book because I didn't know how to continue. I was walking along the beachfront in Durban and saw the thatched roofs of the rondavel shelters - a hat! I had my answer and the book took an unexpected change of direction. It had taken control of the situation.

7. Freewrite all over the place. Bits that appear quite unconnected get written, and then a month or so later, the fitting jigsaw piece appears. I heard of an author sitting down on his floor and arranging all the pieces around him and in this way he discovered his entire novel!

Connected with this freewriting are exercises I give to my novel writing classes. For really good work, a three or four-month novel class is hard to beat, with weekly sessions each of three hours.

In one novel writing class, I had three very different people, one doing a teenage novel, one doing black humour and one writing a relationship book with some Obligatory Sex Scenes. It didn't matter that the people were so different; each one's mind knew the book the author was writing and connected any exercise to his or her work. And later on, these unrelated exercises form an important high point in a novel, and the writer forgets even how they came into being.

I remember giving the students a scene to do when one of them had wanted, in that week's lesson, to explore her character. She was disappointed. They had closed their eyes, quietened their minds, and I said, "You have a dramatic scene ahead of you. Your characters are somewhere and the weather has changed. They are in serious trouble. Just let the scene come into your mind. Get it very clear. Use all your senses. Smell, touch, sound, sight, hearing. Show what's happening. Show the emotions and how they coped."

The student doing a teenage novel wrote a long and remarkable episode where the scuba divers had gone out in a ski boat with a reckless young man who ran out of fuel. He was unable to find them when the weather changed and a gale force storm, with grey skies, choppy seas and spraying mist, broke. The father helped his teenage daughter to have courage and together they made it by swimming slowly back to the shore. The scene was slipped into the story and later became an important high point.

I would also give ideas like "It's a dark evening and there's a fragrance in the air. Now there's a sound. Let your scene come in to your mind, and then just write it."

Nobody expects a perfect product when you write in this way. You will produce a draft, which may need several rewrites. But the work produced has all the qualities of literature. It will be original and uniquely your own creation.

So, though this may seem unwieldy, don't worry about the second part of getting it *right*. Find a computer student or a secretary to type it out *as it is*. This is vital. Nothing must be changed without the author's permission. After it is typed, you can do a cut and paste, and more typing. You can contact a literary agent whose reader may give opinions, which it is wise for you to mull over and to work upon; but the publisher is the person in the end who is your real concern.

Then of course there are always publisher's changes. These you have to accept. You need to be professional and realise it's not you that's being criticized. It's your work and you haven't done it properly. When you look detachedly you will often see that what an editor or literary agents suggests makes sense. Other suggestions you may not like and you can negotiate with them but when it comes to being published the boot is on the other foot. The publisher will have the right to the final say.

Remember, as I have said, that creative work is not pattern writing, but whereas the pattern book has a prepared market, the original creative work may not have one, and you are going to have to find a publisher who believes in you. This will require the help of an editor and a recognized literary agent: publishers don't like looking at work that comes without the guarantee of a high professional standard.

Novelists are pleasantly surprised when the edited manuscript comes back from a literary agent with suggested changes.

"I agree with every one of them," said one of my students who had finished a novel and had sent it off for editing. "And I liked the comment that said it is marketable."

Further good news was that a publisher in the USA liked what he saw and wanted the first full three chapters. This is genuine progress for a writer.

On a Sunday afternoon, in peaceful surroundings with no domestic interruptions, not even a telephone, three of my "old" writers meet at umSinsi House and we work on our novels.

It goes like this.

Arrive, 2.30 pm, a bit of chat and laughter for fifteen minutes. Then, go right-brained with breathing and watching the mind to clear it of thoughts. Then nobody talks for an hour, the dancing pencils are in movement. For these people, it is easy to enter the world that they are creating. They are old hands at right-brained writing.

With their permission, I am giving you an extract of raw writing, done without thinking or any pre-planning, from each of them. All are using novel writing method number 7, of just freewriting whatever happens to come, with no criticism or input from the left brained critic.

Written a few weeks ago, this piece of raw writing is an extract from *Aloes and Opals*, by Shirley Bell, which is still to be published.

## ALOES AND OPALS

It was still early morning when Marjorie set out.

The sun had begun slowly to accumulate warmth and beam it down upon a wintry earth. It wasn't enough warmth though to reach through the layers of Sienna's body as she came to the door of the hut; more like a promise hinted at and ultimately withheld. Sienna felt a little like those stray dogs who came out of the bushes in the early morning beside the mud huts and curled up hopefully in the thin sunlight. It seemed they too had nothing to look forward to. It seemed that life would be the same today as yesterday but still with a survivor's instinct they sought out the sun, feeling perhaps that God would sight along a sunbeam and focus in on them, His forgotten creation.

Sienna heard the thin sound of the baby's never-ending querulous wailing, and could not find enough energy in her legs to rise and attend to her. Petrus' wife had died when the small Lindiwe was born and now she was the only reminder Sienna had left of her sons far away on the Johannesburg mines. It was a dark secret city by all accounts filled with evil, where people forgot the old ways and sons took town wives who spent all their money, leaving their children in the kraals to wail like Lindiwe and Sienna in their loneliness.

A few early morning flies settled on the dung left scattered by the milk cows, now already grazing a fair distance away, their bony haunces standing gauntly outlined against the greeny-yellow grass in the background.

The aloes among the rocks in full scarlet succulent radiance were the only signs of colour in the winter's landscape. They were beautiful too, the Transkei cattle, each one different, with a patchwork of colours, browns and blacks and whites in different shadings and patterns, they were cows who could become known to you, not like the herds on the farm, where each had the same shape and colour, all of their horns the same length and form. When they came home at night from their wanderings you could see they were not so thin after all and their coats were shiny from the good green summer grass. Their long horns framed their faces unevenly and gave them expression and a name.

Tomorrow she would go back down the hill to the white washed farmhouse where Miss Theresa lived now and enter through the wide wooden door of the kitchen and stand there in the glow of the coal stove and take up her duties again. She must go back now, it was not right to mourn so, all of these years for the death of one tiny white child, not even your own. The sight of Miss Marjorie in the Mayfield lounge had been such a shock. Sienna had thought that it was past now, that she had forgotten, but it was not so and the little Rebecca had risen again like a ghost to follow her around as if she was telling her something. Sienna shivered in the cool morning air; as if she was blaming her, blaming her for letting her die.

It was just that one did not expect it. Death had always seemed just another part of life. Some children were strong and they lived, but on some luck did not smile - some - no one could help it - some died. It was the natural order. Rebecca had been different, that had not been a natural order, white children did not die, not so easily, not when they were not even sick.

It made her scared, if even such powerful people as these couldn't stop it, then how could she who was poor and helpless. What would become of her if even Lindiwe should die and Johannes and Petrus should never come home. What would be the sense of her life if all her children ended without a line.

In the distance she saw her, that one, that Marjorie with her head so tall, and her neck so long, walking straight as Sienna had always known her. Walking strong with sure feet on the rocks and paths, looking up, not faltering. She had come, and everything would be all right after all. They would talk and Rebecca would be laid to rest.

The second Sunday afternoon book writer is French born Paulette Barker who is a well-known painter and art teacher. She has had numerous solo exhibitions in the main galleries in South Africa as well as in Paris, France. Her art workshops for adults and children are very popular. A mother of five children she achieved her artistic career later in life.

"I feel that it is accidental," says Paulette, "that I concentrated on my painting first before I became a writer as for me the difference is the media. I sense that when I write, I paint and when I paint, I write. I simply express my inner world and experience of life using two different languages - the one being paint, the other words. With Felicity's magical approach to teaching writing, I was able to open my writing box and let it flow."

In "*17, Quai d'Isly*" which is a book about Paulette's childhood memories, she describes the house where she lived in France and writes:

**17, QUAI D'ISLY**

Grey, tall and sober, this typical French house is no different from the next or the next one. Shoulder to shoulder, sharing a linking wall, they become one. Same height, same double slanted slate roof, same size garden laced by a black wrought iron fence, running along the pavement. It reminds me of a piano. When you look at the notes they all seem the same: black and white, born in the same bed. It's only when you touch the notes that the sound appears. Then everything changes and a new world emerges. "No 17." A gas lantern chats to the front gate. The one warming the darkness of winter's evenings, the other inviting you to enter ...

Jabulani Hlabangane is our third Sunday afternoon writer. He is freewriting a novel called *The Chamelion's Trick* (still to be published.) Here is a sample of his freewriting:

**THE CHAMELEON'S TRICK**

Nobert's father leaped into the air, howling like a jackal. He raised his hyena's tail as he fell on his knees and began to roar the slow lion roar. He placed a rectangular mirror on his square Impala hide mat. From his black medicine bag he fetched a small brown plastic container with a yellow top. He opened it, took a pinch of the tobacco that was inside, and held it to his big nostrils and sniffed at it. He gave a thunderous sneeze and mumbled some words. Nobert's father then took out his bones and threw them on his "magic carpet." An array of bones and shells fell on the ground as he recited something incomprehensible.

Even if you just write a book to express yourself, to have fun with ideas and characters, with no intention of publishing it, you will experience a real sense of satisfaction. It is your world, you are the stage manager, and you are directing the play. So if you have the urge to write a book, then go ahead and do it! All the basic information that you need to get you started is in these pages.

And if you read the books recommended in the bibliography, you will learn a whole lot more, making it quite possible to write a book - if you want to.

## Chapter 13: Freewriting and Poetry

This short chapter on poetry needs to be included. I am not a poet myself but I know that freewriting can unlock poetry in writers. To get more words out of people, I use a method that Peter Elbow gives in his book "*Writing With Power.*" In a chapter called *Poetry as No Big Deal* he explains that advanced poetry has rules of rhyme and metre. He suggests discarding the sophisticated rules and replacing them with simple rules of one's own. For instance, to write a string of lines all starting with "I remember" is one of his suggestions.

Do this quickly without thinking. This works! It broke an eighteen-year-old writing block of published poet Charl Fregona who freewrote the following poem:

**I'll Remember, I'll Remember**

I remember, I remember, the fifth of December.
I remember my dad, a borrower, spender.
I remember the love he exacted from me
And I'll remember then to extract it from thee.

I remember, I remember, the fifth of December.
I remember my mother, a giver, a lender.
I remember the love she squandered on me
I'll remember, remember to give it out freely.

This poem was included in a volume of Charl's poetry published in 1996 as *Moments with Radiance*. UmSinsi Press in 1998 published *Handspun,* a book consisting of words and images by well-known Cape Town artist Elizabeth Vels, and edited by Charl Fregona.

In 1999, Charl again was the Umsinsi editor of a collection of poetry and art in a beautiful coffee-table hard-covered book called *Collaborations.*

## Chapter 14: Adults' Writing for Children

When I teach adults to write for children, I change my whole approach. First, I get from the library a wide selection of books that are written by what I feel are the very best authors. For the young reader, I like to study the work of Babette Cole and that of Pat Hutchins, both top British writers

I say to my students, "Can you see why these books have been published and why they are popular? They're up-to-date with current thinking and they're alive. Every word matters, and their dialogue does all that dialogue is supposed to do. It is apt, in character, and pushes the story forward. It's economical but not bland. There is humour."

In stories popular with children there is often a subversive touch. Because younger children, however adorable, are primitives. They're honest, and social graces are not yet polished. They laugh if you trip and fall in the mud. Their sense of humour is quite different from ours. So is their keyhole view point. A teacher told me she'd read the start of Ann Fine's *Diary of Killer Cat* to her grade 3's. She said that they'd fallen off the chairs, laughing, when she read the start of the story with the cat stating that it's a *cat*, and Hang it, it's *supposed* to kill birds. Which brings me to outlook.

A child's outlook and that of an adult is quite different. A child dropping clothes on the floor in a hurry to get out of them and into play clothes is not untidy. He or she is just in haste to get on with life in the big exciting world.

There's also subject matter. Children are intensely interested in everything around them. The way he or she thinks is quite different from the way that adults think. My four-year-old granddaughter told me my well-written story (from an adult point of view) was *so* boring whilst adults had found it well constructed and excellent.

Adults like it if you can weave in the fact that a child must be honest and not tell lies. They like to bring up other moral issues but children are totally against being lectured to. You have to remember the most important reason for writing is to entertain. Children love humour. They love to laugh.

We know that, as children's writers, we are to show the "corrective." This is a sugar-coated pill to show the child that a certain way of doing things is not good. In my 'Wild Swarm', for instance, the big extravert boy gets a bee sting for being too daring. This hurt and his face swells. That is to tell children that bees are dangerous and to be handled with caution, and in the correct way.

Next to Tolkein, Roald Dahl is perhaps the most popular children's writer. Roald Dahl, I have read, is unconcerned with the corrective and he works with the subversive urge of the child to be a non-conformist.

In a similar vein, there was the story of the good little child who got eaten by the wolf because she had so many medals for good behaviour that they clanked as she walked.

Kids love this 'trouble' for the good children, so remember all this when you are writing for children. Also remember that kids like to be scared. It's also important to study what is popular, not only in books, but also on CD animated books and on television and films. Don't however manipulate your stories. Get deeply into your character and let the character direct the story.

As I have said, please note that this book is more for insights and unlocking of the right brain than it is for exact techniques. There are many good books to help you here. Joan Aiken's *The Way to Write for Children* is an excellent example.

In the past I have given full-length courses of four months on children's writing and novel writing. This, in 1998, produced for one student, four books. Three of these were published by umSinsi Press.

Right-brained work is quick, though of course, it doesn't happen by itself and students have to make schedules for themselves that include writing.

Let us look at the cover of *The Cat-Witches of Stinkfeet*, a

164-page book with large print and a number of black-and-white illustrations, published by umSinsi Press and written by Gillian Gorman.

> The town of Stinkfeet had lived in deadly fear of the seven witch sisters that mercilessly ruled their town for eighty long miserable years. The people of Stinkfeet had no option but to remain living in the town as a spell of Stinky-feet and Bad-breath had been cast on each resident at birth. These seven witch sisters each owned a cat, which reluctantly assisted them in their evil spells and potions.
>
> Sick and tired of being unfairly and cruelly treated by their witches, the Witch-Assistants, led by the ginger cat Jessica, rebel and abandon their witches to start their own Cat-Witch School where only good magic would be practised and taught. Topdeck, a shy two-toned black and white cat, then makes an important discovery, which could save the people of the town of Stinkfeet of their miserable existence. The future of Stinkfeet looks brighter until the witches, discovering their Assistants' betrayal, vow to get revenge ...

Let us also look at an extract from the book to see the way in which Gillian has fostered child interest.

> Jessica was a ginger tabby cat with a bib of white fur and four little white paws. Jessica had brilliant green emerald eyes and would have been quite a breathtakingly beautiful cat if it weren't for her skinny, undernourished and overworked little body.
>
> Jessica was so tired; her witch had bullied and overworked her all day. Her eyes started to droop as she slowly stirred the thick bubbling green brew in the huge cast-iron black pot. Her face was dripping with sweat and huge black rings circled each eye from days without food or sleep. Jessica struggled to keep her eyes open. Eventually, exhausted, she let the long wooden ladle slip from her paws and it was sucked down into the thick green brew. The thin exhausted Jessica slid down the side of the pot into a heap of ginger and white fur on the cold stone floor.
>
> A little while later Jessica was woken up by a pointed steel capped black boot kicking her repeatedly in the ribs, again and again and again. Startled she let out a blood-

curdling scream.

"Get out, you mangy useless excuse for a cat," Agnes the ugly witch screeched, her face reddening in anger and the veins in her neck sticking out, "and don't you ever set your grubby little paws in my house again."

Awful Witch Agnes was the ugliest witch you have ever seen in your entire life. Think of the ugliest witch, times her ugliness a million times over and you will get Awful Witch Agnes. She had a whopping bulbous nose that was covered in huge lumpy warts. From each wart grew thick abundant spiky black hairs. Wispy black oily hair covered her head and her body was enveloped in mountains of pasty white fat. She had what looked like one eyebrow stretched across the top of both of her evil muddy brown slit eyes and her thin colourless lips were twisted in an evil smirk. She wore a dirty long back dress that covered her fleshy body from head to toe and a black crooked pointy hat sat perched on her ugly fat head.

Awful Witch Agnes was known for her extraordinary sense of smell but poor sense of hearing.

"It would be my pleasure, you ugly old hag of a witch," Jessica spat and stalked angrily out of the witch's house. She held her head up high as she made her way down the narrow garden path, but as soon as she was out of sight she clutched her stomach as stabbing pains wracked her body.

Jessica was glad that she no longer had to work for the mean and ugly old witch but she was also very scared, as she was now homeless and destitute. Jessica slowly limped down the road to the home of her friend Bluebell. Jessica leapt onto one of the windowsills of her friend's home, her ribs crying out in pain, and waiting until Bluebell was alone meowed softly to get her attention.

****(From *The Cat-Witches of Stinkfeet* by Gillian Gorman, published by umSinsi Press, 1998, ISBN 1-919721-72-X )

In another four-month children's writing class, Jabulani Hlabangane produced his first simple story that we decided was publishable. Called *Samson's Surprise,* it maintained the writers' voice.

At that time, we had Saturday workshops to discuss the adult writers' work that was coming up for publication. Jabulani in his quiet voice, read his story.

The story ends, after a python has unwound itself from the child and disappeared into the bushes, with the woman's husband returning to find out what is wrong as his woman was making such a commotion. The answer from the woman is a quiet, "Nothing."

Now the writers present wanted a much more dramatic end. One person other than Jabulani understood. "Back to harmony," she said. "The danger is over. Nothing is wrong. Correct?"

Jabulani, adamant this was the correct ending, nodded his head in agreement. Yes, in his culture, nothing *was* wrong. The danger had gone. No other ending would do. I allowed him to end the story the way he wanted to. The design and typesetting was sponsored by the Bartels Art Trust, and umSinsi Press published his first children's book.

In another story that umSinsi Press also published called *Themba's Hope*, Jabulani wrote about a deaf youth who saves his lion friend by suggesting to it that it pretends to be dead. The deaf youth then carries it back to the huts and earns a reward for capturing the lion. He gets the reward even though the lion is still alive and rushes off from the place.

The Europeans said, "That's wrong! He should not be rewarded for cheating the King!"

Jabulani replied, "But in our culture the King's word is his bond. He promised twenty cows for the capture of the lion. The boy brought the lion. The fact that it is still alive is not as important as the King keeping his word."

So *Themba's Hope* was published the way that Jabulani had created it.

## Chapter 15: Teenagers, Fiction and Poetry

Besides school workshops, at umSinsi House I run a once-a-week on-going workshop for children. This used to be for the junior primary age group, but some of the junior primary children who have been with me for two years are now high school students, and I notice a change in my class ratios. These days the writers are mostly teenagers, with the oldest at seventeen, and a number of fifteen-year-old young adults.

Working with these young people is indeed a privilege because they have the tools of good schooling, and are ready to explore the freedom of the right brain. I honestly do not know where their stories come from, or how they can be so good, just with a ten-minute exercise on freewriting, to unlock this world for them. The variety of work is equally incredible: one young adult is writing a play for her class, all in rhyme, two others are writing relationship novels, a third is doing poetry, a fourth comes out with a new original story at each free-writing session.

I have also, not without trepidation, published poetry for my weekly students. I am not a poet myself and simply accepted what the children wrote, and which sounded all right to me.

The young people take enormous care with their work, and do illustrations to show the meanings. I told them that they are lucky because they can create a book exactly as they like and I will publish it for them like that. I am proud to say that their poetry has been applauded and I see teachers hanging onto books of poetry by twelve-year-olds because they love the work so much.

Here follows a poem from *"2 Cats and 12 Poems"* by Eva Jackson.

LIE-IN

Sunday morning
Quarter-past eight,
It's morning still
But getting late.
The sky is grey and pessimistic,
I'm still in bed, not futuristic.
The duvet's warm, and so's the cat;
There's not much to be getting at.
A book, an empty coffee cup -
What kind of idiot gets up?

**** *(From* 2 Cats and 12 Poems *by Eva Jackson, published in 1999 by umSinsi Press ISBN 1-86900-147-8)*

What I actually provide is a protective place for what I feel are to be authors, script writers, film directors and poets of the future. This I do by allowing them to express their ideas in a non-judgmental and non-critical environment, and by encouraging their ideas, the latest being a junior writers' circle newsletter to share their ideas, writing tips and some of their work with other young people in schools. They are writing superbly well and I am so proud of them.

One young poet was enthusiastic about my supporting my role. Her mother is a professional editor and she says she always has to drag her work away from her to avoid having it edited. Once it was published, with her own lovely watercolours and drawings, it was publicly acclaimed.

This is because I know that we are keeping the writers' *voice* and allowing them to develop in the way that is right for them. I say to parents and teachers, "Please don't impose adult standards and judgements on children's writing."

In my course, I decided that I would give people confidence during that first lesson so that they knew they could be, and are, writers. That they could use a pencil and write.

And just to show that there is a difference between how the left and the right brain function, I enclose a very short piece of freewriting in the form of a poem (done by right brain methods), about what happens in the learning of English at school (a left brain method). This is also by Eva Jackson:

**English class**

Alliteration - consternation
Onomatopoeia - fear

My intention was that my course would get a person right-brained and writing. It would also protect that writer and provide a nurturing environment until he or she was strong enough to take the criticism of the harsh outside world. I would pick up and dust off writers who had come to grief.

Just recently this happened to one of my fifteen-year-old writers who had her first taste of what a 'real' editor would do to her book. It had totally demolished her. She would have been finished as a writer, had she and her mother not turned up, unannounced, at my door.

I reassured her. "An editor is in a position to give an educated opinion but it is a subjective opinion. Another editor might see the whole book differently," I told her.

"And the best thing you can is to detach yourself from the book, pretend it isn't yours, and read the comments without emotion. If you agree with them, you might like to do what the editor suggested.If you don't agree, then leave it the way you have written it."

I told her that she was lucky that I was her publisher, because, though I always do a small bit of final editing, her book would be published basically as she wanted it. (I remember reading in a writers' magazine: musicians don't have their work changed. No one dabs another lot of purple paint onto an artist's work (or shouldn't) but all along the way the writer has people suggesting changes and improvements and giving comments.)

This is how I protect my students.

My student was happy and back on track. She finished her book. It was published along with the work of other students at a launch a few months ago. She was interviewed for the newspapers and went on television. A writer had regained her belief in her work.

## Chapter 16: Primary School Writers

Children learn quickly. They understand, "Ten minutes without stopping at all." Once the writing and the story gets hold of them, they go on long after the ten minutes. The seven- to twelve-year age group love these creative writing lessons where nothing is taught. They learn freewriting, are told that a story is about someone or something in some kind of trouble, that it takes place somewhere, and the story person has to get out of trouble by the end of the story. Then they are put in touch with their senses, and experience, in their imaginations, smells, sounds, tastes, feelings and sight.

After getting "right-brained", they then proceed to write wonderful original stories in total silence. This surprises the experts. I remember Clive Read from SABC TV-2-Nite coming to put on television this method of writing, and the resultant published books.

I said, "There'll be nothing to see. Just silence and a lot of pencils moving."

"Surely you teach beginnings, middles and endings?" he said.

"Not at all," I said. "Children have read, or have been read to, since they were tiny. They *know* these techniques without being taught anything at all."

The story that follows was written by my granddaughter Genna when she was alone with me and she had looked long and hard at a carpet in my lounge: from the patterns on the carpet she had an experience where the story came alive and she was there, where it was all happening. She was nine years old and she wrote for about an hour and did three-quarters of the story.

I said to her, "Now just don't talk to anyone about your story or the way it goes on. You have a magic tortoise inside you and it will finish your story for you when I see you next."

It was a month before I had a chance to have her on her

own. She finished the story which starts as follows:

**THE BIG GREEN MYSTERIUOS PLACE**

One day I was going for a walk in the Berg when I came upon a gate.

On the gate there was a note which said: *The Green Garden.*

There was also a knocker on the gate, so I knocked on it.

Nobody came so I went in. I found myself in a nook along the path where I picked some guavas that grew on the side of it.

I discovered a fountain. I had a clean little plastic bag with me. I filled it up with pure water. Then I turned to go.

I saw a little path and, tacked onto a tree was a note. This is what it said:

"PICNIC SPOTS DOWN HERE"

so I took that path.

It went this way and that way. I started when I heard someone say, "What is your name?"

I turned quickly but all I could see was a bush. I thought a person might be in the bush because there was no one in front of me. I looked into the bush on my left.

There was no-one there. I looked into the bush on my right. There was no-one there either.

Goodness gracious me, this is spooky! I thought.

And I went on. Then I heard the voice again. This time it said, "Please answer me."

So I said in a trembly voice, "My name is Genna. Who are you?"

"I am Mother Nature's child."

"Then where are you?"

"I'm in the bush on your left."

" I don't see you."

"That's because I'm made out of nature."

"Oh, sorry!"

"Not a problem."

"Then come out onto the path so I can see you."

"I can't because I don't have toes. I have roots. I live in the earth."

"Oh, just wave your arm and I will pull you out and we can play together. Then, at the end of the day, I will put you back."

So, when the wind was not blowing, she waved her arm.

I pulled her out.

She was beautiful.

Then she called, "Mother, Mother."

A voice said, "Yes?"

"I am going to play with my new friend, Genna."

So off we went. She showed me all her Nature brothers and sisters and all her Nature friends.

**** (From: *The Big Green Mysterious Place* by Genna Chorn, umSinsi Press, 1997 ISBN 1-919721-20-7)

These techniques also work for "problem children."

I have also been brought attention deficit disorder learners in a private capacity and I have found that when they can see nothing in their heads, in other words, when their imaginations are not activated, they write nothing.

One small girl called Fatima taught me all of this. She was having problems writing things down. I told her to close her eyes and to write one thing from each of the senses. She opened her eyes and for smell, she wrote "smoke."

I took just that one word, and asked her to close her eyes, take a breath, watch her thoughts and then to put the word "smoke" into her imagination and see what was happening. She sat with her eyes screwed up for a moment or two. Then suddenly she opened her eyes and a smile lit her face.

"Fire!" she said, "There's a house burning!"

"Then write about it," I said.

She proceeded to write a full page in logical sequence of an event in which the mother and father both died in the fire and the fire brigade came along. This proved to me that if you can activate the imagination and you don't stress the child about spelling, they will write. In fact, after four sessions of this work with me, the previously concerned parents told me the child was off her medication for all subjects except for maths, and their delight was real and evident.

What I enjoy is the imagination that a child has.

Here is the start of a story which was freewritten in a holiday workshop that I ran.

**THE ZEBRA WITH NO STRIPES**

In Africa in a beautiful savannah where the grass was golden, the water was cool and sweet, where the sun was as warm as a heater and the trees spread out like umbrellas, was a zebra and he was the handsomest in the land.

One day he found a stain on his coat so he took a bath but it wouldn't come off so he made some stain remover and washed himself with it.

Afterwards, he looked at his reflection in the lake and got a huge fright. He had no more stripes!

"Oh no, what'll I do?" he cried. "I look like a hideous beast! I'll go and ask Cheetah for help!"

**** (From *The Zebra With No Stripes* by Sian Jones, Umsinsi Press 1999 ISBN 1-86900-144-3)

This charming story is beautifully illustrated and the young author really gets into her characters because when the Zebra gets his stripes painted back on him by mouse, it tickles and so he giggles.

If we are talking about imagination, then what about an extract from *The Dogopillar* by seven-year-old Jessie-Lee Redding of the Convent of Our Lady of Natal, Bluff, Durban: this story (published by umSinsi Press) was recently read out over East Coast Radio.

**THE DOGOPILLAR**

Once upon a time there was a little girl, called Anna, who lived on a farm. She had a small brother and three big brothers.

They all teased her because she never chopped down the trees like they did.

She felt so embarrassed.

So she went into the yard and tried to chop down a tree, but she could not. Her brothers started teasing her.

She felt so awful that she ran out of the yard and into the woods.

**THE DOGOPILLAR**

Written and illustrated by
JESSIE-LEE REDDING

She ran and ran.

Then she heard something. As she ran the sound got louder and louder.

She walked a bit closer to see what it was and she saw it. It was an alien. It was half dog and half caterpillar.

So she said, "Heel!"

Surprisingly, the thing came.

She said, "I will call you...Hmm? What shall I call you? I know! Jimmy!

The thing shook its head.

"I know, since you eat trees, I'll call you Dogopillar."

They went home together.

**** (From *The Dogopillar* by Jessie-Lee Redding, umSinsi Press 1999 ISBN 1-86900-158-3)

Of course, the little girl solved her problem and cut down many more trees than her brothers did, with the dogopillar's help. All ended up well, however, as she gave each brother the egg of a dogopillar so they had help with their tree-cutting when their dogopillars hatched!

These are just three short extracts out of a wonderfully exciting range of children's books, written by children for children, and which would be a great asset anywhere in the world that children need simple illustrated stories to read that are written, for the most part, in English.

All the stories may be viewed on (and ordered from) the website http://www.umsinsi.com.

## Chapter 17: Children's School Workshops

It is only for the last two years that I have been doing children's workshops where vast numbers of learners are present. I first started with the junior classes of high school where the results were magnificent.

But schools with learners of all ages came to me for my classes. At one stage I was willing to give the workshop to children in as low as grade 2 but didn't think that grade 1 could benefit. At the Engen Project last year (See chapter 31) all the schools begged me to also give their grade 1's a creative experience, and so I did.

"If you can't write, then draw whatever comes into your head," I said. The children had just a half-an-hour workshop and were as silent as mice as they scribbled and drew away on their papers. I stood by the door as they went out, looking at their pictures. One small boy had a jumble of lines.

"What's that?" I asked.

"Drowning," he explained succinctly. Now I knew for sure that what they were drawing was meaningful for them.

This year, I have gone even lower down the school ladder, to the Scrummies, or first year of schoolers, prior to grade 1.

I don't think there's any time when it's too soon to start stimulating the imagination. These methods work wondrously well for the big majority of children, starting from five years of age. With adults, I tell them the "Why's" of the right-brained exercises.

With children, I am as concise as possible. I know they have a short attention span. First I start off by showing them some books that I have written. Then I tell them I'm not so clever, young people their age are also writing and publishing books and I show them some examples from books that I place on a stand for them to see.

Then I say, "Now let's forget about the books. What we are going to do today may seem as if it has no point, so that's why I have showed you the books. You're going to practice writing exciting work, which could lead to publishable stories. Today's lesson is not in place of any lesson, it's an extra.

"If you like writing, then get a book and do this at home every day and you'll become very good at writing. However, I have rules and they go like this:

- write for ten minutes without stopping
- no thinking
- no crossing out, rubbing out, using typex, tearing out the page
- these are things you'll like. Spelling doesn't matter, nor does punctuation or how you write. You can't make a mistake because this is non-judgmental and non-critical. No one is going to criticise anything you write.
- it's quantity we want not quality
- write "go, go" or "up, up" a few times to keep the hand moving if you run out of ideas
- write anything you like as you start. It may be a poem, a story, anything - but don't think first. Let it choose you. You could land up with something like scrambled eggs but that's okay too.

I say, "You are going to write to music. First see you are comfortable."

Often these workshops take place in the hall with almost two hundred learners, and the teachers are amazed as the children lie, legs waving, and write silently, pages and pages of work. I can see by their body language that they are enjoying it too.

Then comes the reading out aloud, using a microphone. This is extremely popular and again teachers are surprised as the "weak" students who produce nothing under normal methods are eager to read out the work they have done.

This freewriting is the first thing that I teach and then we proceed to the next example, that of atmosphere. And after that we come to character and to story.

With *story* I say, "Stories are about trouble, it's happening as the story starts and the person who is your hero has to get out of it or solve it somehow, and things are different at the end. Your hero can be a girl, boy, animal, bird, plant, something you can't see, something from in the sea... and your story takes place somewhere. Use your senses, give us the sounds, the shapes, the colours and so on. Let the story choose you."

Again, if story is begun in the first session, they can continue with it when others are doing the second examples. If the session on background and atmosphere brings a story *and* a character, that's all right too.

But if none of this has happened yet, by the time we get to the last exercise, that of *character*, there isn't a child that doesn't write a story they have never heard, seen, or had read to them. This means that each child writes an original story, but I insist that they don't write anything that ends "And it was all a dream." And when the story is written, they pick a title and very apt these titles are too.

There is great excitement in reading one another's stories, which are scribbled in bad writing; it doesn't matter. Then I say to a teacher, "That's getting children to read. You do it first by getting them to write. They'll become interested in spelling because they want to spell better. This simple story writing will lead them to reading in the library, and eventually to enjoying the discipline of study."

There's much more to it than you can really imagine, and the results can be very powerful and dynamic. And it certainly makes a teacher's life much more interesting as the stories the children write come from their hearts and their feelings rather than from their heads and their thoughts which are the mechanics of the left brain.

This writing and reading is all based on trust, first in oneself, and then in the group. They need not read out what they have written unless they want to because of the nature of the writing that is done.

The subconscious creative writing muse or higher self is easily hurt and will retire and will not come out to help. This non-judgmental, non-critical way of writing builds self-esteem. The child feels good and capable and worthwhile, not because of praise but from hearing what he or she has written when writing very fast and without thinking. It's good, far better than you'd imagine since it wasn't planned and thought about.

Of course the work is not perfect because of the way in which it is written. Practise will help. But certainly a whole lot of things do happen.

Just imagine if you are a young school learner who is having difficulty with achievement. The child struggles, tries, is criticized and feels sad because of the failure. A bit of the person shrinks and cares less about trying

Schools that care holistically about the child notice the brilliant smile, the look of relief, on such a child's face when I say, "You aren't going to be criticized in this lesson. Nothing you can do is wrong. Spell as you think it is, don't mind if that's not the proper way, write what you wish, the only thing is, don't stop your pencil moving."

Schools are also amazed to find spelling is better; the use of language is better. Learners don't write "*And* this, *and* that, *and* the other." They write interesting complete compound sentences plus they make correct use of dialogue and other dramatic techniques like real old pro's.

Just why is this?

Nobody knows really.

Doing right-brained creative writing leads to many other things such as:

- unlocking of creativity
- getting new original idea
- sorting out problems
- it is therapeutic
- it finds the writer's "voice" or way of using words.

• in geometric progression it improves the writer's ability to put words on paper

• these increased powers of the right brain spill over to the left brain area. My students get 94% at school for English, have academic pins, and do well in maths and other subjects.

Creative right-brained work answers not only the quest for better writing, but for scientific discoveries too.

To complete this chapter on Children's school workshops, here is an extract from *Dimension: Arthropod Terra* by Vlad Buzdugan (aged 13) of Park View Primary School, Durban, who was among a group of grade 6's and 7's to have, for two terms, a weekly session of right-brained creative writing from me at their school. The result was that, in August 1998, these twelve young people all had beautifully illustrated books published and launched at their school.

**DIMENSION ARTHROPOD TERRA**

There was a slight breeze and I could smell wild flowers and hear water coming from somewhere. I started walking north-east and in no time at all I was at a medium-sized stream. There were wild flowers everywhere and the water in the stream was very cold, clear, and refreshing. There was a pretty big dragonfly sitting on a wild flower and I walked up to it to have a closer look.

It was blue, four wings, and ... what's this? A belt? It was a belt, no question about it! And it had a little gun attached to it!

I leaned over to have an even closer look.

"Hey! Keep your big, fat, beady eyes to yourself, human!"

I screamed and started running away, but before I had gone three steps I froze in place and couldn't move. The dragonfly flew up to me and zapped me again with its ray gun. Now I was shrinking until I disappeared completely and reappeared in a dense jungle. I look cautiously around and saw the same dragonfly as before ... only this time, it was as big as me!

"Don't be afraid human, I won't hurt you," it said, twitching its mouth-parts.

"Who are you?" I asked shakily.

"I am known as Split-Wing here in Insectopolis."

"Where am I?"

"You are in my world, Arthropod-Terra. You are, as you would call it, in another dimension."

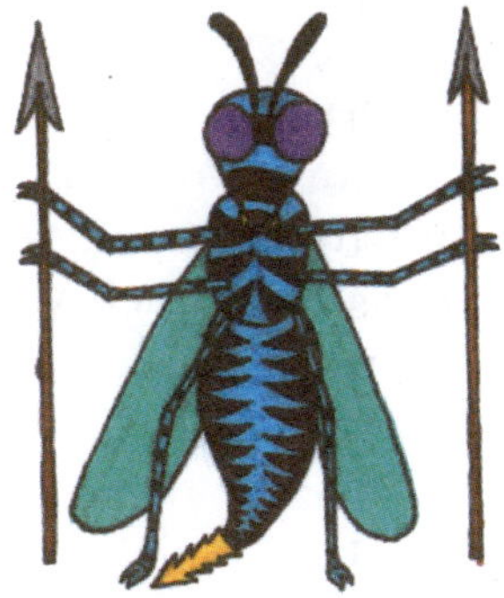

"What! Take me back to where you found me!" I felt like an insect that's been captured by a human, pleading to be let go, only this time, the bug had caught the human.

"Enough talk, I'll get straight to the point of why you are here," the bug said looking a bit annoyed, if that's possible for a bug.

"Well, what do you want me for?"

"You must help me destroy the Wasp-o-pods."

"How do I do that?" I asked quizzically.

"You're a human and an expert on getting rid of bugs, I thought you of all species would know."

**** (From *Dimension Arthropod Terra* by Vlad Buzdugan published by umSinsi Press, 1999, ISBN 1-86900-015-3)

I have done a good many holistic creative writing school programmes which start with a school staff workshop, go on to pupils' workshops, and end with a school book launch of the best stories. A great deal of work goes into it from the pupil's point of view, not to mention the teacher in charge of the project, and the school itself. But the result is a thrilling occasion. It is also great learning experience for young authors who will have a totally different relationship with every book they ever see on a library shelf or in a book shop.

After all, they are authors, too! The benefits are enormous. I'm as excited as the teachers, and the schools and the children and the parents and the educationists.

I'm excited too that next year I've been invited to do workshops in schools in the OFS; and also in the Northern Transvaal where the languages are primarily Afrikaans and Venda. Books can come out in any language a school, and pupils, are proficient in, which means that regional writing and regional ways of thinking and dealing with life can all be preserved.

I'm also excited to have been asked to participate in the KwaZulu Natal Independent Schools Conference of African Literature which will take place in mid-March in the year 2000.

## Chapter 18: And Drawing Too

Schools say, "Please let the scrummies have this creative experience." (The scrummies are the children in grade 0; the youngest in the school.)

I am an evolving document myself, learning more about the process which found me, rather than which I found.

So I agreed that the small children, five-year-olds, can take part in this experiment. They cannot yet write, but they love to draw.

We keep the language very simple.

"Do you know how long ten minutes is?" I ask.

That's a long time to them. They know ten minutes, and round-eyed, they nod.

"Well, for ten minutes you are going to draw and not stop drawing," I say, "and you can draw just anything you feel like drawing, in any way you wish, with any colours that you feel like using. Do you understand that?"

Yes, they do.

"There are certain things you can't do. You can't rub out or cross out, or stop. Or look at anyone else's work or talk. Because you can't keep drawing for ten minutes and do anything else."

They understand.

"Right, I'm going to use music, and before we start, I want you to not think about what you will draw. Let the idea just pop into your head. To help you, we are going to do three things.

"First, are you comfortable? Now close your eyes and pretend you're going to sleep. I want an idea to pop into your head so listen carefully. With your eyes shut, let's do some deep breathing."

We do that, and then I say, "Keeping your eyes shut, look and see what you're thinking. Look to see where your thoughts begin and end. Now wait, and an idea will come into your head. Just look and see what it is, then open your eyes and draw it, and have fun."

They have crayons or colouring materials and they just draw and colour in what their imaginations show them when they have their eyes shut. At the end of the session they show their pictures and tell their stories.

I watched an obviously hyperactive child in a school in Pietermaritzburg leaping backwards and forwards to a bowl of crayons near to him, but he never said a word. Instead, all his focus was on the colourful drawing he was doing. One should never underestimate a child's capabilities!

I have again visited that school, this time to launch six books that the boys had written with the press present and saw the excitement of the boys as they were told that their books would be available to the public at Pietermaritzburg's well-known bookshop, Shuter and Shooter.

My welcome was genuine. The staff have internalised all that they learnt at a staff workshop. Children who couldn't write before, do so now.

Children do not write "plastic" stories, and the grade 1 teacher told me, "The grade 1's are writing wonderful stories. We have given up using dictionaries, and the stories just flow."

# Chapter 19: Teachers' School Staff Enrichment Workshops

School staff enrichment workshops are among the workshops that I like best, perhaps because they are a challenge and perhaps the hardest kind of test for the right-brained methods.

This is because teachers in junior schools go to educational institutions that teach them the way to teach "creative writing." They teach beginnings, middles and ends.

I have been at schools where a teacher has said, "We can't get anything out of these children. So don't expect much." Amazingly, some very original and publishable stories have come from these same children.

That teacher then said, "But that's the way we got taught at training college. Beginnings, middles and ends."

So, into the staff-room I go and look around at the faces of perhaps twenty-nine staff members, finished after a hectic week of work in a junior school.

The staff are too polite to say what they feel, but I have heard someone mumble, "I teach Maths. How is this going to help me?" and a male teacher will tease a colleague who is obviously the physical training teacher, about getting to know his inner self.

I start with the information about the left brain, the critic, the know-it-all, and so on. Then I move over to the fact that there is this huge silent all-knowing partner just waiting to be called upon. I give them the rules. Ten minutes writing, no stopping, no thinking, no crossing out, no keeping control, you can write *up, up*, or *go, go.*

There is some amusement at this, but, I say, "You must keep on writing. And writing *go go* or *up up* helps to keep this flow." I explain the need for music, being comfortable, and getting from the beta to the alpha state which requires some deep breathing.

"After that, please listen closely to me. To activate your

imaginations and to stop thinking, you need to simply watch your thoughts without doing anything about trying to stop them. Then, when you are not thinking anything at all, open your eyes and write the first thing that comes into your head and keep going remembering it is quantity and not quality that we are after."

We start and I notice at first a tenseness in the face and body, then imperceptably comes the change that I know will come. They have moved over the creative side where time doesn't exist and they are enjoying themselves, the pencils say, as they dance over the pages.

After the ten minutes is up, there is a small glimmer on some faces. No one wants to read. I know teachers are private people, so we move on to the use of freewriting in doing journalism.

Very quickly, we go over the requirements of "It happened to me," "My story," "Last page" or similar things teachers may find themselves writing which could be published and paid for, and which staff can teach to their pupils. Of importance is the catchy title, the catchy first line, the look of *dancing journalism*, a neat end, and no more words than the slot demands.

Next is the use of freewriting that they have just practised in story writing. We consider the fiction techniques of character, dialogue, background or setting, and plot. Two that I never take any further are plot and dialogue. "If you get your character right, your plot will follow."

First I deal with setting and the senses and they are told they are to use their senses in their heads and that they are going on a holiday, anywhere, and they are to really *be* there. They are not to pick the place, the place will pick them. And here is where the whole thing changes.

I notice smiles on faces, and a whole change in body language. There is no fixed time for this exercise and I watch to see when the majority are finished. Then I ask who had a nice time, who was really there, who smelt and felt and tasted, and the excitement is tangible.

There is a whole happy feel of laughter and lightness of mood in the staff-room and the tired staff are on a "high" which they admit, and say things like, "I had prepared it at home but my right brain took over." Another had begun a serious poem, and then she'd got light-hearted and had had fun.

Someone said, "I was really at the beach, enjoying the tranquility and the sea and suddenly this herd of wild horses with flared nostrils, snorting breath and stamping feet, came charging along the beach. I got such a fright, especially as I was so tranquil."

I did more imagination exercises which I have found to help students who are given topics in exams and feel hopeless about what to write. I can remember feeling like that when I was at school, all those long years ago.

"Let's try a topic," I said, "Let's just say, 'My school holiday.' That, given to a student in a test, is likely to bring up some deadly dull work. But please close your eyes and take a big breath and tell yourself you're going right-brained. Now look at your thoughts. When you aren't thinking anything special, put the words 'My School Holiday' into your imagination and just watch the images that come into it. Use your senses again This time, don't write anything. This is just to see how much more exciting writing can be when using the imagination and the right brain."

They closed their eyes and sat there, then opened them. Again, smiles and nods. Yes, amazing things had turned up. Different, colourful happenings.

It was coolish outside. "Now I'm going to show you something else," I said. "How to stimulate children's imaginations. Please close your eyes. And watch your thoughts. Now you're somewhere that it is hot. It's getting hotter. It's actually very hot indeed. You can feel all the feelings of somewhere hot. When you have experienced as much as you wish, please return to this room and your present state. Then open your eyes and just let's hear where it was and if you experienced anything."

Yes, they'd been at the beach, in the desert, in an engine room, in lots of hot places and had smelt the smells and heard the sounds.

"You won't overwrite. You just see where you are, and who is there and your pencil will do the rest, " I said.

And this is about all that a mixed staff, on a Friday afternoon, is prepared to work through.

At the end, I was listening to comments such as, "I hate writing. I didn't want to do this. But I'm going home to write. It was marvellous."

Another said, "I feel so energised. So light!"

Yes, you get energy and power when you work right-brained. The feeling of being 'high' and positive and on top of everything is normal.

Staff also know this creative writing the children are to do is never for marking. It is just for listening to. Already they were impressed with some classes of children who, immediately after the creative writing lesson, were already neatly writing out onto sheets of paper the work they had written rapidly, and were correcting their punctuation and spelling.

"You see," I said, "they are doing it because they *want* to and not because you said so. This is *educe*, education, leading out of a person, not imposing anything upon them; it is this latter which children resist and which makes teaching difficult."

This right-brained creativity could bring a story with a *character* in the first freewriting session. Let the student write it through all the sessions. But by choice, I never do *Character* before *Background* because you might have just a character, action and story but lose all the nuances of setting and atmosphere.

It is rare for staff to read out what they freewrite; I am grateful to Clive Beetge, on the staff of Clifton Preparatory School in Durban, for allowing us to publish his freewriting on *atmosphere* which was done at their staff enrichment workshop in August 1999.

**A NEW MORNING**

Along the whispers of drifting cloud, carried by the slightest breeze, a warm, moist scent drifted lazily upwards. A warm glow was slowly filling the cool, calm morning air. The sun was rising and slowly fading the dark to light.

Through the morning dusky haze, the far-off amber glow of the log cabin lights shone peacefully and warm. The woods creaked and stretched as they began their day's toil. The birds already long awake chirped and glided as a gilded boat off a shingled shore. The swirling, curling column of smoke from the kitchen chimney indicated a new fresh beginning. The bubbling brook, somehow, called out to the waking frog to take a morning splash.

The Jones' were bashing around the kitchen after a battle of switch on switch off sleep, pacing passages and gentle rocking. The beauty of the outside world seemed somehow alien and strange to them, since their world had been turned topsy-turvy and totally upside down. Yet not for all the jewels of the world would they ever change a thing to go back to the old drudgery, rat race life of yesterday.

It seemed almost impossible to even imagine living before that so very special day. That day being ever better than creaking, stretching woods, even better than a frog's morning splash, even better than the rising curling smoke or even the gliding birds...That was the day of days...the day that they were blessed with a son.

A son, gurgling, smiling, laughing, crying, eating, poohing but yet above all living...That was the day of days. The past night's sleeplessness faded into a blissful memory with the first morning smile of a happy contented baby.

Life is so very, very good. Up, up and away we go, for tomorrow will soon be today, and the future will be the past ... the day after that will be school, varsity, marriage and after that ... a new morning.

*(After free-writing this, Clive Beetge typed this out and gave it to his wife who had just given birth to their baby son.)*

## Chapter 20: Creative Writing Workshops For Adults

The writing that I have heard from students in workshops that I run in various places has made me so envious. How I wished I was in the class instead of running it! How, I have wondered, *how* do I get all this information out of myself and into a book to help writers, and people interested in writing, everywhere? I probably would still be enviously listening to students and wondering who was going to be my mentor and unlock my creativity if I hadn't run a workshop for the Johannesburg and Pretoria Writers' circles in Bryanston, recently.

Dee Andrew is a Johannesburg writer who flew down to a writing weekend at umSinsi House in 1996, and as a result, had a book called *Mindscapes of the Nineties*, edited by Peter Strauss, published by umSinsi Press in 1998. Because of this book, she gave a talk at the Bryanston Library, and the result of this talk was that I was invited by the Bryanston Library to run a weekend workshop for the Johannesburg and Pretoria Writers' Circles in the library at the end of August 1999. The programme was put together by dedicated writer Julian Mitchell. I flew up and was met at Johannesburg airport by Dee Andew with whom I stayed. Saturday morning saw us at the library.

Fourteen nervous, left-brained people, from different walks of life, separated out from one another, were there at the start of the workshop. The workshop was to run over two days. Each student was to write a story after the Saturday lesson and bring it to the Sunday workshop.

I did my usual. I handed out the pieces of paper and they wrote the things they felt about themselves. This is always an icebreaker. Barely a soul can write competently with their 'other' hand. I spoke a little about the other hand; of how it can prioritize things for a person; of how it can only tell the truth because it homes into the real person and its needs.

When you don't know what to do, ask questions with your dominant hand. And answer with your non-dominant hand.

"When I have too much to do, I do that," I said.

We continued. I told them I am only a facilitator, that I use teacherless methods which mean that they read (when they want to) to hear what they have said and not for criticism. We went through the techniques for getting over into a right-brained state. I put on the music and they wrote.

Because of what happened for everyone that weekend and also because it brought about my *knowing* that the birth of this book was upon me, I asked permission from Julian Mitchell and Johan Erasmus to include pieces of their raw writing in their own handwriting; these were unplanned freewriting. As I have said before, this is not necessarily the finished product, but with practice one becomes so good that the material often cannot be improved upon.

Those writers, that weekend, wrote real stuff.

"Writing needs courage. It's like getting undressed in public. People want to know how it really was, what it felt like. They don't want the glib and the plastic."

There were tears in some cases, and not only from the writers. My eyes were bright with tears in a couple of instances as well.

Just before starting to free-write, Julian Mitchell wrote down the following comments as I was talking:

- Start with atmosphere: setting
- Character will follow
- Smell touch taste sight hearing
- Use all the senses.

Here is his ten minutes of freewriting:

> Standing on a concrete block on top of a kopje under the blue sky. The concrete beginning to burn through the sole of my shoes making my feet tingle. Getting bloody sweaty now.

Time to stop for a while as shimmer getting too bad to see far away.

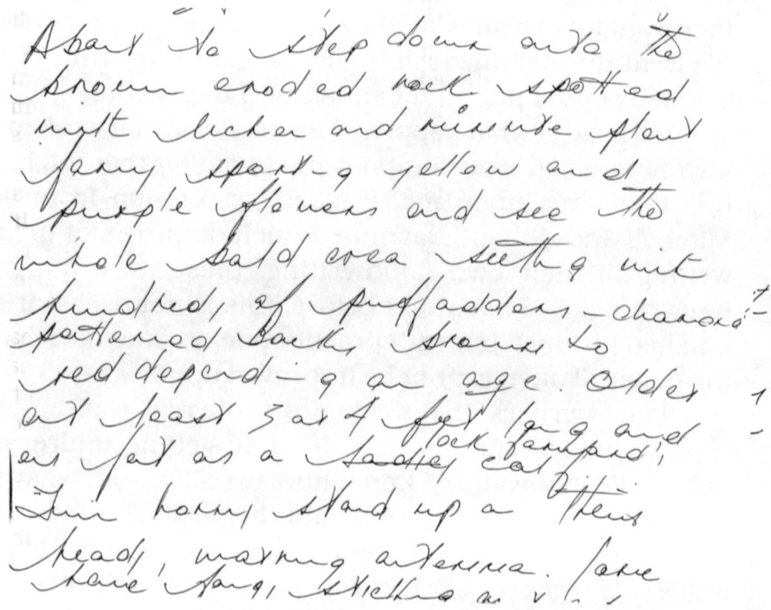
About to step down onto the brown eroded rock spotted with lichen and minute plant forms sporting yellow and purple flowers and see the whole bald area seething with hundreds of puff adders - diamond patterned backs, brown to red depending on age. Older at least 3 or 4 feet long and as fat as a lock forward's calf. Twin horns stand up on their heads, warning antenna. Some have fangs sticking out

About to step down onto the brown eroded rock spotted with lichen and minute plant forms sporting yellow and purple flowers and see the whole bald area seething with hundreds of puff adders - diamond patterned backs brown to red depending on age. Older at least 3 or 4 feet long and as fat as a lock forward's calf. Twin horns stand up on their heads, warning antenna. Some have fangs sticking out of the sides of their mouths. More are coming, slithering inch by inch from the fringe of bushes and grass.

Decide to stay where I am. My bladder is full. Wonder what puff adders will think if I pee. Who cares - no one can see me. Rocks are hot pee is hot - they won't know the difference. So I piss on them. Small revenge. I can feel the sun boring into neck and bald patch. Getting thirsty now. Shouldn't have pissed on them. Snakes revenge I suppose. My water is hanging on a branch at the edge of the rock. Looking at it makes my tongue, furred, stick to the roof of my mouth.

Torture myself by looking at the water pouch perspiring on the branch through the theodolite telescope. The lichen is a different grey from that on the rock. Hang on - millions of blood ants snaking down the gnarled branch onto my canvas water bag. Little buggers - hope they leave some for me - most probably into my salami sandwiches. I like them when the salami sweats in the sun. Squeeze it and little fat specks pop out like zits on a Saturday night before the jorl. Satisfying. Sit down on the concrete slab finding the shade of the blazing white pillar. Have to keep moving round like the hour hand on a church clock when you're waiting for your bird to arrive when you think she's run off with someone else.

Shadow is now reaching over onto the diamond backed snakes and they ease away from the shade. The sun hangs massive over the purple horizon drawing the snakes towards it like water on a hot stone. Much like my piss sizzled on them earlier.

Then the snakes are gone without even a whisper - like they'd arrived.

I tip-toe over to my rucksack doubled over in pain.

(WRITTEN IN ABOUT 10 MINUTES.)

After lunch we did character sketches, and chatted about *story*. We had lots of input. And whilst I encourage writers to be flexible and to be able to write by hand, and discourage creative writing with a computer, Julian had an excellent tip.

"Switch off the screen," he said. "Then you can stay in your right brain."

For the instant that the screen is on, it shows the lines below the spelling errors, and the left brain wants to stop to correct things. I came home and tried that myself and it works.

This next piece of writing is exactly how Johan Erasmus freewrote his character exercise. He is a journalist by profession and apologetically e-mailed me to say that he had not polished it at all. That is exactly how I want it, because this is a book that lets you into the secrets of writers before the work is polished, edited and published. This is so that you know that you, too, can produce your excellent work of whatever kind that is right for you, if you access your right brain as I have shown you and then, later, polish your work.

Here is Johan's freewriting:

(1

She was walking along the little dirt road towards the village, crossing some open savanha grassland. The wind stirred the grass and she could smell spring was in the air. It was all Jane's fault the villagers had said, she thought, thinking back about the event of the past three months. Jane was responsible that village life had disintegrated ~~she~~ from the way it had always been. The women protested against their tasks, against the men, against anything rational, traditional. In turn the men had to let them go and eventually found that they themselves were losing their inhibitions

She was walking along the little dirt road towards the village, crossing some open Savannah grassland. The wind stirred the grass and she could smell spring was in the air.

It was all Jane's fault the villagers had said, she thought, thinking back about the events of the past three months. Jane was responsible that village life had disintegrated from the way it had always been. The women protested against their tasks, against the men, against anything rational, traditional. In turn the men had to let them go and eventually found that they themselves, were losing their inhibitions and becoming a freer society. As for the kids, they just had fun. Yes, she thought, the new schoolteacher, Jane, changed the village life here in Malawi, broadening everyone's mind.

(Johan went on with his story, finishing it for the session on our second day. Here is some more of the story.)

The fact that she did not think about the outcome of this is indicative of her state of mind. She entered the village and found the senior elder sitting in front of his hut. "Enjoyed your class today, Jane," he said, looking up at her as he did so, and she could feel that he wanted to say so much more to her; would like to empathise with her. For she is leaving, banned from the village, by the council of elders, for what she had done.

She felt at a loss for words momentarily. How was she to know that the senior elder's son would fall in love with her and leave his wife! She waited for him to speak. He almost did, but as he opened his mouth something got the better of him and he closed his mouth, looking down at the ground. She could feel his humiliation, as if all this was not his fault. An awkward moment developed out of nothing and then a chilly breeze intervened, leaving worries, assumptions, actions in its wake. She suddenly felt cold and turned towards her hut. She thought about what had happened.

Moses, the senior elder's son, was part of her class of people from the village she had come to teach English. Once she had gained their confidence, and they started to like her, the teaching came easy and they made progress. Except for one that is. Moses.

During the day, I did *back in time* exercises, and

*imagination stretching* exercises: we listened to sounds, then found the spaces in between sounds and writers found another dimension to the art of listening. There are many of these exercises in Marilee Zdenek's book, *The Right Brain Experience.*

This was a really special workshop: it was special because of the people there, the work that they produced, and the whole feeling of the weekend. It was extra special to me because it precipitated this book.

But workshops like this can happen, just as beautifully, in other places, and in different ways.

They depend a lot upon *serendipity.*

## Chapter 21: Writing Marathons

"Don't forget we've got a marathon on Saturday," I say, speaking to a writer whilst we are in the company of non-writers. I forget the effect that has on people until I notice the puzzled looks I get. Of course, I am talking about a writing marathon, not a running marathon.

Surprising as it may sound, physical work is not as difficult as mental work. Mental work requires work at a physical, emotional, mental and even spiritual level. People are really exhausted after a hard spell of writing, even though they have enjoyed it.

I notice this with the children and when their parents come to fetch them, I say, "Your child has worked really hard. We've had lots of breaks but you'll see, she has written a whole book of her own and illustrated it as well." (Parents will often tell me that a younger child will go to bed and sleep the whole afternoon after a full morning's workshop.)

Marathons go in this way.

A number of writers, any number even forty or fifty, sit with paper and pencil ready. They hear that in a marathon there will be four sessions of writing. The first is ten minutes of non-stop writing. Then people will be given the chance to read what they have written. Again, no one has to read though it's better for them to do so as soon as they feel they can. No one may comment on anything that is written. This is because it gives the person who wrote it the chance to hear it without comment.

After the first session, the second session will be double the length. People will write for twenty minutes, and then will stop and again read out. Then people may comment on work read out at the *first* session. It's rather tricky when there are a number of people present and you'd love to say something at the first reading but can't until the next round. If there are a lot of people present every fourth person can read out their work (or a part of it) at each reading session, which gives everyone a chance to be heard. These are the rules and marathons *do* work.

The third session is for forty minutes, and the last one for an hour or longer. So in a marathon, participants can expect to write in total for more than two hours.

The work that people get from themselves in these two hours goes to a very deep level and will give them material for perhaps a whole year. There is material for short stories, poems, bits of books - all sorts of things.

Of course, the marathon is started in exactly the same way as any freewriting session. People get comfortable, close their eyes, breathe, then watch their thoughts, and start writing as soon as they have a calm mind. At which time the music starts.

Whilst talking of marathons, I must mention a weekend when seven of us, five of whom are now actively writing at a professional level, went away on a weekend workshop to a cottage in the Byrne Valley in Natal.

It was a *writers'* weekend. It was freezing cold. We slept on the floor as there were no beds. But we wrote. We did marathons, and also did a simulation of a Zen walk when each just walked, alone, very quietly, and very slowly, very slowly indeed, using all the senses as if they were out on antennae so that each one saw, smelt, heard, and felt much better than usual. Then, when they were ready, they just sat down and wrote. Some shared their work, some did not. But that is what this kind of writing is all about. It is deep and what the writer writes, matters to him or her and will therefore matter to those who read it. I recommend marathons to all writers who have come to understand the freewriting method and to use it as a way of writing. They can work very well for children as well.

Frances Roberts produced this piece of freewriting which came from seemingly nowhere, after the "Zen" walk.

**Extract From Free Writing Done On A Writer's Weekend In The Byrne Valley. Later Became Story "Flight Of Freedom" Published In Personality Magazine.**

Betty cleared the dishes while Megan sipped her coffee slowly. It made no difference that it was real, the aroma of roasted mocca java still clinging to the air. She listened to the kitchen noises, water pouring into the sink, dishes clattering. I can't do it, she thought. Not now. This woman has been so good to me. She'll die. She'll just curl up and die. She looked towards the passage where it lay, white, flat, accusingly, the address and name in bold black letters, plastered with colourful floral stamps. She wondered where he was, now. She hadn't looked at the postmark. "I'm going for my walk." Betty stood in the doorway, her ginger curly hair sticking out over her ears, making her look a little wild. The "my" got to Megan. Not that they went together often. It was just a little separating gesture. She couldn't help wondering how they would separate out their possessions if the worst came to the worst. She looked out of the window. There was a patch of light behind the clouds where the sun was trying to break through. Take your umbrella she yelled. Too late. The door had slammed shut as she said the words. Megan drank the last of the coffee, put the cup down on the table and went to watch Betty's figure retreating go down the path. The light brown leaves made a vast carpet across the lawn so that you couldn't see the patchiness any longer. She felt envious of Betty. Everything seemed straightforward for her. She could just stay where she was, no decision to make. No letters to open. That was the truth of it. I'll get dressed first. As if dressing would give her some protection against his words. In her pyjamas she might feel vulnerable. Somehow when she read his letters, it was almost as if he was there, watching her as the words poured out. Carefully, Megan traced the line of her lips with the brush, then took a lipstick, and brightened, and filled in the rest. She tied her straight, long blonde hair back with a black whatsit and picked up her crystal, looping it over her head. God, she thought I must be crazy. He's miles away, he can't do anything to me from there.

The following is part of the story which, after polishing, was eventually published in *Personality Magazine:*

**FLIGHT OF FREEDOM**

Megan was in a turmoil. The letter had come in the evening post. She had not dared to open it last night. It lay there, in the passage, on the carved Chinese dresser, where someone, probably Victoria, had placed it, the night before.

Victoria had made the breakfast. Megan ate it, woodenly, tasting nothing. The muesli could have been dry leaves, the toast cardboard.

"I see you haven't opened your letter."

"Later," her voice was strained, "I'll open it later." She couldn't hide the angst. Victoria stared at her, a long hard stare.

"So, it must be from him, then."

"I don't know. I'll look later."

"Coward."

"Yes. No-one said I wasn't."

Victoria cleared the dishes away while Megan sipped her coffee slowly. She could taste that it was real, and inhaled the aroma of roasted *mocca java* that clung to the air. She listened to the kitchen noises, water pouring into the sink, dishes clattering. As she swallowed the last of the coffee, she had a vision of a tall man, mop of brown hair framing his face.

"You'll be able to wear a pony tail soon," she had laughed at him and pulled her fingers through the thick hair. He had taken her hands away, put them round his back and pulled her towards him. Their lips met - a light butterfly kiss. There was a light in his eyes, a teasing smile that raised a flutter in her breast.

She shook her head and the image vanished. She was back in the kitchen. I can't do it, she thought. Not now. Victoria has been so good to me. She'll die. She'll just curl up and die. She looked towards the passage. The door was open and she could see where it lay, white, flat, accusingly, the address and name in bold black letters, plastered with colourful floral stamps. She wondered where he was, now. She hadn't looked at the postmark.

"I'm going for my walk." Victoria stood in the doorway, her ginger curly hair with its grey streaks sticking out over her ears, making her look a little wild. The *my* irked Megan. Not that they went together anyway, normally. It was just a little separating gesture. She couldn't help wondering how they would separate out their possessions if the worst came to the worst.

She looked out of the window. There was a patch of light behind the clouds where the sun was trying to break through.

"Take your umbrella," she yelled. Too late. The door had slammed shut as she said the words. Megan drank the last of the coffee, put the cup down on the table and went to watch Victoria's figure retreating down the path.

The light brown leaves made a vast carpet across the lawn so that you couldn't see its patchiness any longer. More were falling from the enormous oak next to the house. She felt envious of Victoria. Everything seemed straightforward for her. She could just stay where she was, no decision to make. No letters to open. That was the truth of it. *I'll get dressed first...*

As if dressing would give her some protection against his words. In her pyjamas she felt vulnerable. Somehow when she read his letters, it was almost as if he were there, watching her as the words poured out and confronted her.

Carefully, Megan traced the line of her lips with the fine lipstick brush, then filled them in with a darker coloured lipstick. She tied her straight long blonde hair back with a black bow and picked up the rose crystal, looping it over her head. Heavens, she thought, I must be crazy. He's miles away, he can't do anything to me from there.

**** (From *Personality Magazine* and *South African Short Stories Volume 3 Roots* published by umSinsi Press, ISBN 1-919721-17-7)

Frances Roberts also produces a quarterly writers' newsletter with very useful marketing information and help for writers. Her contact address is:

PO Box 35210
Northway
4065.
South Africa
E-mail : francesr@iafrica.com
Tel/fax : + 27 31 563897.

## Chapter 22: Help for Home Schoolers

Right-brained creative writing can also provide help for home schooling parents. Twenty-four mums came to umSinsi House for a two-hour workshop. Their reason for being there was they had taken over the duties of the teachers in the classrooms and were providing their children with good schooling.

I admired these busy young mums. They had to do tests for starch and bisect insects for biology and teach maths and of course, they had to teach creative writing which comes into the syllabus. They too had come with books of unlined paper and their pencils.

I used a different approach. They needed to be able to impart knowledge to their children, so they needed to know the same as teachers need to know and they also needed child language to be able to impart this knowledge successfully to their young.

So I told them that the left brain tries and can fail, and that the right brain doesn't try, it just does. It cannot fail because there is no failure.

It is unwieldy but has brilliant original contributions and uses language in a better way than the left brain and because of the need for non-stop writing, it helps the slow and attention deficit children who have to keep their pencils moving.

I explained that the left brain is the *learnt* side, that it is the one that school and society sharpens and prepares for life's work, but that the right brain is the home of creativity, music, art, and religion and has a holistic approach to life. I explained that we need a whole brain, but this contribution only comes afterwards; it might be necessary to do a small amount of editing once the child's work is read out.

At this point, the child often wants to write it out and correct it him or herself anyway. I also mentioned that these creative writing books the children write in are not for marking, and they are private.

We then did our ten-minute session of freewriting, followed by a session on *atmosphere,* and then I touched on *character* which leads to *story.*

"*Story,*" I said, "is about trouble. Something or someone is in some kind of difficulties or trouble and needs to sort it all out. A story takes place somewhere, and seasons and weather and the senses come into it. And that is all."

I explained that for the child, everything is to be kept simple. They don't need to know the complexities, just simple instructions. Very simple ones. And that they are quick to understand what is wanted of them.

Six months passed and I received a phone call from one of the mums asking me to speak to advanced "Home Schoolers" at their convention.

She asked me to give them a lot of information about the right brain creative process.

I asked her how she was getting on and she said, "Wonderfully well. My sons of eight and ten both love their creative writing sessions. And I've thrown away all the notes I had on beginnings, middles and endings. I just do settings and use the senses, like you showed us."

I was very interested in this feedback.

## Chapter 23: Workshop for APEK 1997

I ran a workshop for thirty-two teachers at APEK - the Association for Professional Educators of KwaZulu Natal, who told me they were the only union really doing much in the field of professional development - (that was in 1997.) This was to be a four-hour workshop. I was mildly daunted. Teachers with their knowledge, and developed left brains are not exactly the easiest of audiences.

I explained the right and left brain, the critic and so on. They did freewriting sessions and *character* and *back in time* and *fantasy* exercises.

At the end one teacher said, "It's my fault, I see now, that I get thirty boring essays every week. I've not been stimulating the learners."

Another said, "Thirty boring essays! You're lucky! I get one hundred boring essays every week."

I was pleased some six months later, to get a phone call from one of the schools present. Four of the teachers had been at the workshop. The school wanted a workshop for the full staff as the teachers from the APEK workshop were getting excellent work from the pupils. The school was having some work typed out and sent home to parents who were delighted with the results.

Yet another six months or a year later, a young man came bounding up to me when I was shopping in the local supermarket.

A teacher at this same school, he said, "You won't remember me, but I was in your workshop at APEK. My whole teaching approach and method has radically changed because of it."

## Chapter 24: Empangeni Educational Department Workshop 1998

A telephone call from Mrs Zethu of the Empangeni Educational Department (Examinations) brought about a workshop in Empangeni. We would be met there and accompanied to Ngwelezanele Township hall about five kilometres away. The trip to Zululand would take about three hours, they said.

This was another test. This time, fifty educationists that included school inspectors, head masters and headmistresses, members of the Educational Department and a great number of teachers from schools in far-flung areas around Empangeni were present, with pencils and paper. They were mostly Zulu-speaking people.

Again, I did my talk about the critic who would be out at lunch at this session, and the great big sleeping partner in the right brain who would be accessed and I explained the need to write without stopping for ten minutes. Unfortunately I do not have any of the material that was read out when the first session was over. But I do remember what the answers were.

"How did you find that?" I asked.

"Interesting!" was one reply. The gentleman in question then read out an eloquent tribute to his mother. There was a lyrical quality to all the work that delighted me. Amongst these teachers were some who said they would also like to write fiction themselves. Fifteen teachers asked for workshops in their schools so that their learners could benefit from right-brained creative writing as they had done that morning. Another workshop would one day take place, they said, enthusiastically, amidst much clapping.

## PART THREE : THE OUTSIDE STORY, FROM INSIDE

### Chapter 25: Introduction to Part 3 - Simultaneous stories

The story of this next section, of writers' successes, must run parallel to my own story because, without the one, the other would not exist.

Way back when we used blue ink and "G" nibs at school, and there were no fans, overhead projectors, computers or Internet, I was an excellent student. But only once in all my school years did I get asked to read out an essay. That was the day that the British Royal family toured through Durban, waving to the crowds. I was amongst them, and so excited was I to see a real King and Queen and two Royal Princesses that the essay I wrote that weekend was read out to the class on Monday.

Though I loved reading, I had no interest in writing, until I was a young mother with two small children. Then the Writing Muse swept down and snared me. I have recounted my experience with the left-brained structured way of writing, which bored and frustrated me. I again pay tribute to Fay Goldie, ex Fleet Street journalist, who ran every kind of writing class in Durban in the 1960's, all of which I took. I dabbled in various genre, enjoying myself. I turned the many happenings of my life into successful published writing. I learnt photography well enough to do my own photographic illustrations in black and white, and to have my own darkroom. I learnt to paint.

After seven years of freelance writing, I took over the editorship of the South African Bee journal. To my distress, it had no copy to edit. This meant that I had not only to design and to lay out the journal (from which metal printing plates were made) but also to write and to edit most of the copy.

My freelance writing experience helped me, and I

interviewed beekeepers in various parts of the country, went to Zimbabwe to see a bee mating tower, and to Athens in Greece to a world beekeeping conference.

By now the work I had done had changed the image of the journal for beekeepers. From hobbyists, they had moved to commercial beekeeping. I was getting out of my depth so an editor who was a beekeeper with a science background joined me: he was in a position to be of real benefit to the country's growing export market and to their bee industry. My part then was purely as compiler of the journal. This was not creative and after a spell of seven years altogether, I did a University Education Diploma at the University of Natal, left writing and the journal and moved into teaching.

I already had a B.Com degree. With the UED, this meant that I was qualified to teach accounting, economics and other commercial subjects in schools to a matriculation level. Though I loved teaching, and also began a photographic club and took over the school magazine, after several years my bones began to twist. The physiotherapist did tests that proved that I was working with the wrong side of my brain. He told me that I should leave and do right-brained work. That meant *writing*, I knew without doubt.

At the end of that year, I left to work full-time at home at writing. I wrote my first book, which was published by Tafelberg, and then my second book. The first one was translated into Afrikaans and also published. I thought I had *arrived*.

Nothing remains static however, and the change in the country brought about changes for writers. The one hundred-and-fifty-page photographically illustrated true book that I wrote about bees and beekeepers wouldn't sell.

"The wrong book at the wrong time," the publishers told me. A number of children's books I had written were rejected. The Mills and Boon book that would make my fortune got lost somewhere in England.

Sadly I decided that the universe had a strong message

for me. That was - give up writing. To stay in touch with writing, I devised my right-brained course unaware of its power - and how it would bite back at me.

My first course was made up of two friends on barter transactions, and one person who had seen the small advertisement in the newspaper. She proved to me that my course was working. The first story that she wrote was published in a magazine. She found she had a flair for humour and wrote a number of polished travel articles which, along with other short stories of hers, were regularly published in magazines.

I was doing monthly courses, and having a writers' workshop one Saturday a month for any student who would like to bring work to read. The stories were excellent.

"We can't just sit here telling each other how good the stories are," said Ester Lee. "We must do more. We need to go public."

This brought about the birth of umSinsi Press, *umSinsi* being the Zulu name for the *erythrina caffra* or lucky bean tree, that wonderful red parrot-like flower that blooms on bare thorny branches against a blue, blue sky at the end of winter. A provincial emblem, it seemed appropriate as the name for a publishing house for local writers.

I found a literary agent in Pietermaritzburg who helped to keep the writers' voices whilst showing them how to tailor their stories so that they were professional. I used bond money, found a printer, learnt about providing the printer with the origination of the book and getting it on disc, and what was needed for its cover. Our first volume of short stories was launched on Arbor day in 1995.

So local writers planted a tree, metaphorically, when others were planting real trees. Our first book of short stories was brought out in a run of one thousand copies. We had our first launch of *South African Short Stories, Volume 1, Sundowners*, at Exclusive Books in the Pavilion, in Westville. Three months later, we brought out our second volume of short stories, *Cadences*, which was also launched at Exclusive Books.

I had sold some of our first books, but many remained in boxes at home. I had hit my head against the biggest stumbling block of a publisher. That of marketing. I had to keep on going forwards, had to be dynamic. I couldn't keep using capital! I also wasn't a sales person. I was a writer and wanted to remain one.

What could I do?

## Chapter 26: "*That Old Stove*": 1995

A number of years previously, I spent three days at a children's writing convention where I learnt the proper way to write for children. Beginning, middle with three episodes, and ending, all going in a cause and effect straight line from beginning to end with some repetition to make it easy for the child.

Using what I had learnt, I wrote an excellent story (I thought). Preening myself, and to get praise for my credible effort, I read the story to my four-year-old granddaughter. She threw her head back, and laughed.

"Grandma, that is *so* boring," she said. We were standing in my kitchen. She looked around her and made up a story of a stove that ate the food and the pots on top of it, then the cupboards and the sink, then the walls and finally the roof. It was standing out in the open when it started to rain.

I took the story, humbly, added story elements, and sold it to a magazine. They returned it two years later, set up for publication, apologising that they no longer published children's stories. Here I saw my salvation to my publishing problem. It was up to standard. It needed illustrating. I could paint, but my attempts to draw people were embarrassing so Genna, now eight years old, with no hesitation, drew the characters and animals.

I drew the stove which needed arms to get the pots into its mouth (the oven.) The printer printed the covers and before lamination, I, an artist with no knowledge of colour printers, hand-painted every one of them.

*That Old Stove* was to start off all the amazing school publishing activities that I currently do.

## Chapter 27: Manor Gardens Primary School Grade 3 : 1996

*"That Old Stove"* arrived in a box at Manor Gardens Primary School in Durban, where a teacher bought a copy. Unbeknown to me, sixty-three children in grade 3 used it as a prototype to write their own books.

One day I received a phone call.

"Please will you publish our books for us? We have been using *That Old Stove* as our model. We need them done with their illustrations in colour, though."

"No," I said. "I am afraid that I can't do that!"

"Please," the young teacher, Jenny Beeton, said earnestly. "There is a place for children's books written by children. Please."

I demurred, then finally I agreed simply that my granddaughter Genna and I would go to the school and listen to the children's stories. Genna had also just written *The Big Green Mysterious Place* and our literary agent had given us advice, which Genna was contesting. We would share our experiences with these children as well as listen to their stories.

Two classes of Grade 3's sat in the media centre with their teachers. Genna was nervous. It was an auspicious occasion. One of the grade 3's, Lucy Sessions, read out her story called *My Cat on Holiday,* which was about their cat, called Cream, who had, by mistake, gone away on holiday with the family in a caravan.

Then they heard Genna's new story about a girl playing with a plant that was Mother Nature's child. Not confident at that time, I had asked for input from a literary agent who suggested that Genna should have nature sprites as the child's playmate instead of the actual plants. Genna even turned her picture upside down to show that the roots in the ground became hair for the plant when it was out of the ground and had become her playmate. (See page 78)

The children all totally agreed with Genna's story. Well, for market study, what could be better? Here was the market and they had given their opinion. So Genna won her battle against adult literary advice.

At Manor Gardens, the teachers concerned with these books were purists in taking children's work as it was before it was "improved upon" either by siblings, parents or the child him or herself.

We agreed to publish seven of the sixty-three books exactly as they were, with the teachers just correcting spelling and punctuation. In rare places, they would sort out tenses. The books would be published in full colour with laminated covers and with all the glitz of an adult launch with newspaper photographers and publicity.

"Sophie was so excited when she heard that was to happen," said young author Lauren Johnson, "that she accidentally jumped on my foot." (Sophie and Lauren were co-authors of one of the books. Lauren wrote *Sasha's World* and Sophie Troskolanski illustrated it.)

But there was a nerve-wracking journey for umSinsi Press to travel. I had no colour printer nor scanner. The computer had not enough memory or rams. I had nightmares when I heard that Giovanna Cowley, author of *Abby's and Tabby's Adventures,* had delayed her holiday flight to Italy in order to be at the launch. There *had* to be a launch but *would* there be one? I worried.

Then I remembered a dream that I often had where I was on the platform at the station, trying to put all my clothes and possessions into my suitcase in order to shut the lid and catch the train that was about to leave. It was a most disturbing dream. Then one day, I had the dream again. I was on the station, but this time, as the train came in, I calmly put everything into the suitcase, clicked the lid shut, and easily caught the train. I never had the dream again, and when deadlines cause me stress, I like to remember this, taking it to mean things will all get done in time.

Everything did, and with wonderful help from my friend and colleague, Charl Fregona, the books were done and the evening (in December 1996) was one that stands out in my memory as I am certain it does for each of those small authors.

I am pleased to say, that three years later, I still meet for writing workshops with most of this same group, who are now publishing their third, fourth or fifth books. These still retain the same charm of their first stories, though now they are much longer.

Here is a sample of nine-year-old Rachel Baasch's *work:*

**MY KITTENHOOD**

To begin with, I had no name and then when I was six weeks old a human came and took me away from my beloved mother and four brothers and sisters.

I was called Timothy and had to do all my business in a ridiculous cardboard box full of sand. By the end of the day it was quite nasty and smelly. I missed my mother and brothers and sisters very very much.

The human I lived with was called Simon and he gave me tasty treats every day. I loved the imported chocolate that he shared with me.

That was the end of my kittenhood.

**** (From *The Life of Samual and his Brother Blue*, umSinsi Press, 1996, ISBN 1-919721-12-6)

These books written by children were the start of the present three hundred books with child authors that umSinsi Press has published with schools participating more and more in the holistic programme that starts with a staff enrichment programme. Each child is as important as these early child writers. Each launch is such a special occasion.

Today, amongst the books that children have written and illustrated, are stories that are suitable for the very young readers. There are also stories for the sophisticated young teen reader. There are stories for boys and stories for girls.

UmSinsi Press also has books in Afrikaans, child written and illustrated in colour, which are suitable as Outcome Based Education classroom readers. Children's potential is out in full as child helps child! And child fascinates child!

Directly after that initial launch, a few Durban book shops did put some of the books on their shelves and the children were so excited to find them in our loyal book shop, Adams & Co.

The Durban Municipal Library Services also bought a full set of seven books for their Musgrave Road library. The children's excitement was sky-high when they heard that other children were taking out their books on their library cards. I was also told that these books were more 'out' than 'in', showing the popularity of these books with their peers. I still come across young library users who get really excited when they see these books in the library and choose to take them home to read.

About that time, a member of the Department of Education and Culture in Durban found these books in Adams and I received a phone call telling me questions were being asked. "Who is this umSinsi Press?"

Of course, I tracked the official down and showed her the books we were doing. I learnt a lot from her about the books that were needed in schools. She told me the story of the lack of funds for books.

She also told me that the young learners were resisting reading because when there were books, they were often inappropriate. In the cities and townships the Black children were reading the same books as their European counterparts. They did not want books written by adults that were geared towards "Black problems." She also told me that the rural children did not relate at all to life in the city: they needed a very different kind of book with a very simple story.

I received more marketing clues to the South African readers' requirements at a convention at the University of Westville-Durban where I was one of the speakers. Some of the students were angry. They wanted books written about poor lives and misery of the black people, and of violence.

An answer to this, for me, came at this same Convention when I listened to an absorbing talk by a lecturer who said she had had a humble upbringing but today had a comfortable lifestyle. She put it all down to the reading that she had done when she was young. She had read the Hardy Boys, James Hadley Chase, and The Secret Garden, and anything she could get her hands on.

"Let them read widely," she said, "anything they want to."

That morning, I also heard that children in informal settlements dream of better lives when they draw television aerials and steps leading up to a house.

I had heard as much as I needed to about the requirements of people where books were concerned. UmSinsi Press had the green light to go ahead. I would publish beautiful books, books we liked, books with stories that other children and adults liked, never mind if there was a market for them.

We would create our own market with publicity because we know that, underneath the cry for making things as cheap as possible and bringing down costs, people do love beautiful things - and quality does count.

Our books would be the best we could do, on the best paper, with the best finish. They would be a pure art form.

Where the contents of the stories were concerned, we know that kindness, humour and caring, the *real* things of life, must win over violence and crime.

So it is that umSinsi Press is working towards the development of a literature that is South African, that belongs to everyone. That has the voice of the person who writes it. That is the voice of the people.

It is rewarding to know that the National English Literary Museum in Grahamstown is excited with umSinsi's efforts and has many of our books included in their historical record of the development of English literature in this country.

## Chapter 28: "A Matter OF Ear"

In the process of publishing, and in our decision to be "purists" rather than grammarians, I like to re-read Professor William Strunk Jnr. In his book *The Elements of Style*, he clearly tells us that "the claw-hammer he murdered her with" might not be grammatically correct, but it's "a matter of ear." Of how it sounds. And murder is violent. This way of writing endorses the violence.

With authorities like this giving me support, I *dare* to let children express themselves as they wish. I *dare* to remember that people use language in different ways.

A headmaster I was seeing, and congratulating, on a young learner's published work explained to me that the child had used the words "pulling and pulling" and that the teacher had changed it to "he pulled."

The headmaster in his wisdom, had changed it back. As he said, "pulling and pulling" has more of a sense of the drama of saving a drowning child (the hub of the story) than he "pulled" him out.

The headmaster also said, "This is an Indian usage. You'll often find words that end with ...ing being used in our work."

In my period of listening to what was going on in the country where writing and books were concerned, I also remembered a talk given at the University of Westville-Durban by Jaye Heale, our eminent children's writer and literary critic.

"In this country three languages are often used together as a way of speaking. Why don't we find this in our literature?" he asked.

My colleague, Charl Fregona, who had done a course of publishing in her Masters degree, finally decided my path as a purist publisher by supporting the word order of "Me and my brother" which was what Rachel Baash of Manor

Gardens Primary School had written in her story. This had been approved by her school and, I was told in the voice of my objections, that "Chomsky " was Charl's authority. That *voice,* or how people use language, should be respected.

Since then I have done more reading on the subject of *voice,* and keep as nearly as possible to the author's way of writing, being aware of the growth and natural progression of writers.

In fact, it is this "ear" that is the deciding factor in umSinsi's publishing. This works very well with our process of writing fast, and then of listening.

It is in this way that one can see the effect of a piece of writing on a group. What is more, both the writer and the publisher are able to *hear* it.

It really *is* a matter of ear.

## Chapter 29: Launch AT Trevean : July 1996

In July of 1996 we had our third launch of new books, this time at Trevean, the historic home of Brian and Ester Lee, in Bellair, Durban.

The launch was in the billiard room with its superb ornate interior. A good fire for a cold mid-winter's day was burning in the large Victorian fireplace.

Our three new books we were launching were *Moments with Radiance*, a book of poetry by Charl Fregona (with five of my watercolours), Ester Lee's *Mãe*, and my first writing guide, *Creative Writing in Four Easy Lessons.* Three new books. Our titles were growing.

Ester had her own way of writing. She liked to write black humour that was calculated to shock. She objected when the literary agent editing her work told her that what she wrote was not *nice.*

"I don't want it to be nice," she said. "It was like that in Maputo. That happened. Once a train driver saw someone lying on the train lines. He stopped his train, got out and asked the man, 'Is this suicide or have you fallen down and can't you move?' It was suicide, so the train driver got back into the train and continued his journey."

By letting writers have a say in their work they become aware of their own development. This also leads to the discovery of voice, and to further evolution of themselves as writers. UmSinsi Press decided that the place of the editor is to give clarity to the reader through punctuation, spelling, tenses and paragraphing.

Ester Lee is Portuguese. She writes in her second language, English, and her book, *Mãe* (which means "mother") retains her voice.

The first paragraph of the book follows below and after that are extracts from a review that appeared in the *Mail and Guardian* newspaper in 1997, with high praise for Ester's book.

**CHAPTER 1 : THE NIGHTMARE**

He looked at her carefully. Her dirty dress hung on her like from an old coat-hanger. The dress she always wore, from when she had flesh on her. Her thin pale face, still smooth at the age. Her haunted eyes whitened by cataracts, her thin steel grey hair, plaited like a rat's tail, down her back, past her thin haunched shoulders, brown false teeth. But there was still some beauty on her. And that unusual strength.

"My last wish," she said to him "is to be buried alive."

She spoke like from the dead. But she was sitting across the table in the diningroom.

The bright sun of July came pouring in: the sunlight spread into the house, scattering cockroaches, spiders and other creatures with the fear of light.

A plastic tablecloth, which had been there for several years, was now stuck to the once beautiful timber of the dining room table. Some pale yellow small roses printed on it were still faintly visible amongst the bits left from the meals when they had food to eat.

****( From *Mãe* by Esther Lee, Umsinsi Press, 1996, ISBN, 0-620-19835-4)

## Sections from the Mail and Guardian review:

UmSinsi Press in KwaZulu Natal is a tiny publishing outfit which deserves notice. Over the past two years it has put out 23 titles. They seldom have print runs of more than 500, and don't yet make profits. Nevertheless, they are getting into KwaZulu-Natal bookshops and are selling their children's books to schools around KwaZulu-Natal at a steady rate, and now consider themselves an established small Durban publisher.

The owner and moving force behind umSinsi is Felicity Keats, who has been a writer, editor, journalist and teacher for 35 years. The press was born from mixed impulses: on the one hand, the hunger of Keats' regular writing group to see its work in print, and on the other a confusion as to what the big publishing houses were prepared to take on during recent times of tremendous change. *******

And every so often the small publishers who run on love rather than money throw up something extraordinary.

umSinsi may have done just that with Ester Lee's autobiographical *Mãe*. Written by a Portuguese émigré from Mozambique, it tells of her strange and painful relationship with her mother who stubbornly stayed on in Maputo after being widowed, defying conventions of every description by living with her young black, alcoholic servant. It is a fragment of a novel - sparse, disjointed, raw and utterly gripping. Is this a once-off, or a genuine new talent? Certainly worth keeping in touch with umSinsi's catalogue for her next book.

(With acknowledgements to the *Mail and Guardian* Newspaper)

By 1999 umSinsi Press had three hundred titles, most of them by young authors. All the books are displayed on our web site at http://www.umsinsi.com.

Ester Lee has now become an international writer with the complete trilogy of her mother's life in Maputo being published by Minerva in England as *I was Born in Africa*, Minerva Press, 1999, ISBN 0-75410-598-9.

This pleases me greatly. She found her "voice" and umSinsi Press gave her the platform to be "heard from."

This led to her own confidence in her ability and in her unusual talent, and an international author has been born.

# Chapter 30: Flea Market in Durban, 1998 - Pelham Primary School, Pietermaritzburg

The marketing of the growing number of children's books by children along with adult written books was a bother to me. How ought umSinsi Press to market them when printing was done to order, for the most part, from a range of titles?

Try the flea-markets, someone said.

We chose the most upmarket flea market in South Africa, passed its requirements, and took a table. We made a special cloth, got there early, parked miles away and trundled our books there. I also had a small marketing brochure which read

*Creative writing workshops*
*Relax, go further, unlock your creativity,*
*pass your usual boundaries*
*Good for school staff, pupils, adults, children,*
*business people, housewives.*

My growth has been organic, and not goal orientated. Where I am needed, I go. That day, at the flea market, one copy of "*That Old Stove*" for R10 was all that I sold.

It was hot, the toilets were miles away, and then it got windy and threatened to rain. The message was clear. Flea markets were not for me. I still had to find out what was.

Shortly after the day of the flea market, I received a telephone call from a teacher, Jenny Buck, from Pelham Senior Primary School in Pietermaritzburg, who asked if I would come and give a staff enrichment workshop at the start of their next term. We named a price per hour that I would charge. Little did I know what this one workshop was going to mean.

The day came for my first school's staff workshop, but nevertheless, it went off well with my next commission being to teach all their grade 3's in their hall in the school. This way schools could afford me. The cost of an hour's tuition was shared out amongst two hundred children, so for two hours they had a wonderful experience. They unlocked their creativity and wrote *atmosphere*, *character sketches*, and then their stories, to music

I then offered to typeset and originate twelve books and Pelham had their first launch. They chose six pupils who were English-speaking and six who were Afrikaans-speaking. Two of the Afrikaans-speaking children chose to write in English, the four remaining pupils saw the start of our books that were written in Afrikaans.

This launch that they had was the first launch resulting from school workshops that I had given. The children had decorated their tables in the themes of their books. The press, the invited guests, parents and educationists were all saying, "This is *real* education. It's exciting! It's wonderful!"

It also put young authors into the public eye so that they themselves were able to recognise their achievements. This could be a start, at a young age, of a life-time's career.

Pelham Primary School have now extended their range and have brought out eight more books in Afrikaans and four in English. Below are three short extracts from work done by Pelham Primary School pupils. The poem, *Sacrifice*, comes from Liza Wang's first book of poetry published in 1998 and called "*Poems*." She brought out a second volume in 1999 called "*Another Volume of Poems*". Her third book, called *Breaths*, is being launched in November 1999.

**SACRIFICE**

She knew this happened
But not to her,
Her money was supposed
to keep her safe
From the insecure depths
Of poverty.

But she gambled until
She was thrown
Into the tough, harsh arms
Of homelessness.
Her pride keeps her safe
From the lower order.
(She still thinks of herself
as the rich young lady
she once was.)
She will not accept this,
She won't live it.
She's spent too many
years trying to escape.
Inside she knows there's
only one ultimate conclusion.
She is still proud
As blood flows from her wrists
And she sacrifices herself to class.

**** (From *Poems* by Liza Wang, umSinsi Press 1998, ISBN 1-86900-012-9)

One Pelham Primary School writer who deserves mention is Nadine Komen. Her first book in 1998, *Flappies Red die Dag*, was in Afrikaans. Nadine has moved across to English medium instruction and, in 1999, she had a second book published called *Alien Adventure*. This is how it starts:

**ALIEN ADVENTURE**

"You're an alien! You're an extraterrestrial! You were sent to Earth on a secret mission - to observe Human Beings and the way they think and live and what they do. Your mission is complete. You will return to your home planet, Taiga. We will fetch you at midnight so be ready."

Shocked, you get out of bed and wonder if it was a dream. You don't tell anyone but still pay unexpected visits to everyone you know and greet them sadly.

They look at you as if you are crazy.

**** (From: *Alien Adventure* by Nadine Komen, umSinsi Press 1999, ISBN 1-86900-126-5)

Another short extract follows from a beautifully illustrated book in Afrikaans by Melissa Beukman (Grade 7). Called *'n Vlooi Se Lewe, Aai!*, this humorous book is about a flea who is trying to find the right dog to live on.

**'N VLOOI SE LEWE, AAI!**

Nee jong, 'n vlooi soos ek het sy rus nodig. Laasnag het ek omtrent rondgerol.

Ek dink 'n worshond sal moontlik ideaal wees. Ek wou altyd 'n huis met lang gange gehad het.

Die volgende dag pak ek my tas en "woeps-waps" is ek tuis by my nuwe huis. Ek pak my tassie uit, slaan my bedjie op en lê rustig en slaap.

Skielik rol die woorde "Badtyd!" by my ore in. Die volgende oomblik spoel 'n brander oor my, en prettige borrels sweef in die bad rond.

Ek hoes en stik, en voor ek my asem kan terugkry, slaan die volgende brander my onderstebo!

Na 'n uitputtende gespartel kom ek by my ouerhuis aan.

"Ag Ma! Ek dink ek sal nog 'n week wag voordat ek trek!"

**** (From *'n Vlooi se Lewe, Aai!* by Melissa Beukman, umSinsi Press 1998, ISBN 1-86900-008-0)

## Chapter 31 : Engen project : 1998

I'm not sure how the idea developed - but I became aware of the tremendous benefit that our children from privileged homes were having in getting to authorship at a young age.

Young Jade Fernley aged nine had her second book published, a volume of stories called *The Bad Dream Spider and other stories.* A Sunday newspaper interviewed her and she was photographed. The journalist said to me, "I'm so envious of that young girl. She is writing fiction and is in that world. If I had had that start, imagine where I'd be as a novelist today."

This and other things that happened prompted me to make a proposal to Engen Petroleum Ltd. that I teach in a traditionally disadvantaged school, that they sponsor this work and then publish twelve books of their choice from that school.

David Goldstone, visionary thinker and social investment co-ordinator, took the project much further than that. He drew up a programme for thirteen primary schools (six of them from Merebank, seven of them from Austerville) in the vicinity of the Engen refinery at the Bluff, Durban. This would give every child in each of the schools the opportunity to unlock his or her creativity.

The schools were wonderfully co-operative in finding spaces and timeslots for the teaching, and in providing every child in every school with a small book of unlined paper. In fact, everyone was wonderfully co-operative, the headmasters, the thirteen thousand children and the five hundred staff members alike.

It was education. It was massive. It was daunting.

To begin with, the schools had the project put forward to them. Their part would be to provide a suitable large space for sometimes as many as one hundred and eighty or two hundred students to have a lesson for an hour. They would also supply unlined paper and pencils.

Next came two massive workshops for teachers. The teachers from the Merebank schools had a two-hour workshop in the community hall in Merebank, and another workshop for the teachers in the Austerville schools took place in the Engen auditorium.

This teaching of so many teachers, with the use of a podium and a microphone - and my music - on a stage in an auditorium was another daunting experience.

Some school facilities were meagre. At one school, for four hours, I used a loud hailer in the hot sun out on the playing field where class after class came to write creatively to classical music amplified by loud-speakers.

In another school, there was a security man with a large rifle. I wondered what the circumstances were like there to require this protection service.

For six weeks, accompanied by Jabulani Hlabangane who was learning all that I was doing, (and in the end was teaching in a classroom nearby) we went daily to the schools.

After that, the staff of each school selected seven books and from these, umSinsi Press did book originations and printing began.

Eighty-nine new books were registered with the five legal deposits in the country, each book having its own ISBN number, in a historic programme. Here are extracts from three of them:

**THE STORY OF REX**
**Nomfundo Radebe (8) - Austerville Primary School**

Once upon a time there was a dog at my home. His name was Rex.

He was a clever dog. We used to play with him every day.

When I am back from school, on weekends when Mom sent me to the shop, he used to go with me. I was very sorry when Rex didn't come back home one day.

I went in the shop and I bought milk and bread for Mom.

There were naughty boys.

They called my dog and they ran away and the dog followed them.

**** ( From *The Story of Rex* by Nomfundo Radebe, Umsinsi Press, 1998, ISBN 1-86900-098-6)

This touching, sad tale is illustrated by the young author but it does have an ending that satisfies both the author and the reader.

**WANDA'S GLOWING WISH SOCKS**
**Rowan McAllister (12) - Assegai Primary School**

"No, I don't think I'll take them," said Wanda. "Have you got any green socks?"

"Yes, I have one pair left."

"I'll take those," said Wanda.

"That will be R7,95," said the cashier.

When they got home, Wanda tried her new socks on.

"Perfect fit," said Wanda.

It was raining so Wanda could not go out to play.

"I **wish** it stopped raining," wished Wanda.

The socks started glowing.

The rain suddenly stopped. Wanda was excited and ran out to play. She had all the friends in the neighbourhood.

**** ( From *Wanda's Glowing Wish Socks* by Rowan McAllister, Umsinsi Press, 1998, ISBN 1-86900-082-X).

**THE BRAVEST DOG IN THE WORLD**
**Avinash Singh (11) - Junagarth Primary School**

Then the noise came again, even louder. Bang! Bang! It was right behind him.

But when Percy jumped round, there was still nothing there. He began to feel a bit frightened.

Whatever could it be?

Soon Percy's master came home. The dog was very glad to see him.

But as he was saying hello, the noise came louder than ever.

Bang! Bang! Bang!

Percy's master laughed.

"What a noise your tail makes! " he said. "Every time it wags, it bumps against your kennel."

"So that's what it was," thought Percy. "Fancy being frightened of my own tail. I'm not so brave after all."

**** (From *The Bravest Dog in the World* by Avinash Singh, Umsinsi Press, 1998, ISBN 1-919721-99-1.)

The book launches were next on the programme. The Merebank launch was held in the Merebank Community Centre. The stands for each school that were placed around the hall had had much thought put into them. They were very beautiful with the books published by each school on their own stand, displayed for all to see.

At a long table on the stage, covered with an Engen banner, the dignitaries sat. These included the mayor and the circuit inspector. Children were selected who read from the various books that they had had published: this gave each school a chance to be heard. During the function, each child was publicly presented with a copy of his or her own book, autographed by Mr David Goldstone of Engen.

The Austerville Schools Book Launch followed a similar pattern and was held at the Austerville Community Hall, where the schools had really gone to town with their decorating of their stands. Again, the dignitaries were there, and each child came onto the stage and received the gift of a book for him or herself, and a few read from their books.

At one stage of the proceedings, Collingwood Primary School put on a choral verse that the children had written themselves. In it they thanked both Jabulani and me; at the same time they took us "off."

"Now close your eyes, and breathe," they chanted, "and let your imaginations work. Watch the picture in your head, and then start writing." I knew then that children miss nothing. And that just one session of right- brained creative writing was indeed a valuable gift.

And in another part they chanted as they acted, "And we are authors. We are authors."

Yes, authors who need encouragement and recognition for being in a historic programme. We did get the SABC TV-2-Nite there when the Austerville Schools presented one copy of each of the new young authors' books to the Austerville library. All of the books have been put in a special Engen book site by my ace webmaster, Allan Jackson of Media Group, and can be viewed on http://www.umsinsi.com.

Teachers in both Merebank and Austerville loved the whole project so much that they wanted this to be an annual event. Sponsorhip is not available this year so Austerville Primary School who has budding authors still writing books took it on themselves to hire a bus and to bring twenty-one young writers to umSinsi House where I was delighted to give them a free workshop along with juice and biscuits. One young boy who apparently does nothing in class wrote a good imaginative story. I later telephoned the school and said that umSinsi Press would sponsor its publication.

It is a pity they have not had a backup to last year's teaching to make more books and more proud young authors, so that they could have a launch like last year's. Such wonderful work is encouraged by sponsors - and how we, all of us, children particularly, miss them when they are not available.

It was Jabulani Hlabangane who came up with the next idea. He had been a pastor at the Ark Christian Ministries in charge of the education and social development of street children and was used to thinking of sponsorhip and plans of getting money to help the less fortunate.

Whilst I was puzzling what to do after the Engen project, he said to me, "You've done the work. There are all these beautiful illustrated books written by children. You need now to find schools with no books at all and put the two together with sponsorship money. This will mean that child helps child. Everyone loves children. And the authors and the schools will benefit too from the royalty payments."

That put a whole new programme together in which the KwaZulu Natal Education and Culture Department came to select books that were displayed at umSinsi House. Between their Durban South and their North Durban areas, they chose sixty-eight books that were of the correct standard for use as classroom readers.

We needed sponsors and I started looking for them. Our first sponsor, Consumer Credit Holdings, donated six thousand rands. This exciting donation meant that we were able to give forty-six sets of four books to the Durban South region along with twenty one copies of Cecile Levin's Nativity Play, *A Special Gift*, ISBN 1-919721-69-X. This play with music for young children, complete with audio tapes, would enable each school to put on a Christmas play.

I had heard how they lacked amenities and I said, "But what will they do about playing the tape?" I knew that the tape had songs in different languages for them to hear, along with a blank side to the tape so that the music teacher could reverse the tape without taking her eyes off her class when they were rehearsing the songs.

"The staff have tape recorders at home and they will bring them in," the education official told me. We had a presentation at umSinsi House with the press present to write articles about the child authors who had it "write."

It was like the bread and the fishes and the multitude in a story of Jesus. The books were to be rotated and used in four rural schools in the Durban South area during the school day. After school they would be kept in the reading centre, and then taken home at night for the children to read as library books.

This was just the start of an exciting educational project. Most of the books the Durban South Educational Department had selected were written by the children from traditionally disadvantaged backgrounds. The subject matter of these simply written books comes from their experiences and they match the interests of rural children in Natal, making them the perfect reading books for children.

We had just *thought* this was the case, but now we know this for sure, because in following up on the work we have done this year, we have probably found a sponsor for the rest of the entire first pilot project.

The Durban South Education Department had said that sponsors were welcome to visit to see for themselves the conditions of the rural schools where, in many cases, children do not have classroom readers for classroom collections. So I invited the sponsor, our photographer, and an official from the Durban South Education Department to guide us "over the hills and far away" to see the schools we will be helping, who, up until now, had just been names.

"There are no tarred roads to the schools," the official told us. "But I will take you to Mid-Illovo Primary School which has text books but no classroom reading books." She added that, to get to many rural schools, we would need a four-wheel drive. "But from the school I am taking you to, I will show you rural schools in the distance. They are all much alike." She added that the District Manager knew of our visit but she was unable to inform the school principal as there was no phone at the school.

We *did* go over the hills and far away.

We travelled inland from Amanzimtoti on the South Coast to Umbumbulu, and then to Mid-Illovo, through sugar cane fields and neat farms, past goats, and small houses, and through misty hills and green vegetation. We went, and we went, and we went.

The cell phones of the people in the car were dead as we were too far from built-up areas.

We finally went along an untarred road though sugar cane fields and arrived at the school. On the side of a mountain, it was large and peaceful, with a cow and a goat grazing on the road outside.

A neatly dressed acting headmaster, who had been in an important meeting to find the right person for a deputy principal's job next year, spared time to show us into a classroom. Grade 2's were sitting at desks, working in jotters, in a large spacious room. There was a blackboard, with written work on it. Here, I thought, is a rural school, here it is peaceful, here are disciplined children, here are people who *want* to learn.

Here they *need* books to read.

We placed on a table a box of fifty-five books that the Durban South Educational Region had selected. First the teachers crowded around to read the books that child authors had written. We then invited the children to come

to the table, and take books to look at. It was just as I *knew* it would be. In seconds, small heads were all that one could see as the children crowded quietly around the table, hands outstretched for books. They stood there, turning the pages, and admiring them. I knew that they were relating to the young authors. Perhaps some were even imagining that they could write a book themselves.

It was time for us to go. The acting headmaster was presented with the books. The sponsor had seen the project. It was a real one. We looked at a winding dust road far below that went towards another mountain and then disappeared. "There's a rural school down there," the education official told us. We chose to believe her.

The sponsor could finance the giving of one book per child in the twenty-one schools in the pilot project in the Greater Durban South Region: this project is just the tip of the iceberg.

*In this same region, another one hundred and twenty five rural schools have no classroom reading books at all.* In the North

Durban Educational Region there is a similar situation. Many more sponsors are needed and this project *must be* ongoing. On each book, the sponsor's name will appear. The schools will retain the books.

UmSinsi Press has full documentation now, the support of the Durban South and North Durban Educational Councils, with their choice of the simply written colourfully illustrated books that they would like in the classrooms. Many more excellent books in the eleven official languages will be written and illustrated by children, and published, as time goes on.

The project gives royalties to schools (where this applies) and to the authors, whether child or adult. All sponsorship donations will be deposited in a special trust fund created for the project. This is in the care of attorneys Austen Smith in Pietermaritzburg with Mr Brendan Cullinan, attorney in charge of the trust fund.

*(Tel: umSinsi Press: +27 31 4641556 for more information.)*

## Chapter 32: umSinsi House 1999

Designed by me forty years ago, umSinsi House was at first a home for a large family with a larger pendulum swing of friends, relations - and writers - and had always been a busy place. Because the happenings where the house is concerned could take a whole book on its own, I'll skip *everything* up to the present time.

Now it is owned by my brother and sister-in-law, Mike and Dulcie Lloyd: they are fascinated at the role the house is playing in providing somewhere that is large and quiet and has the right atmosphere for writers; all kinds of writers.

The peace of the surroundings include the trees outside and the indigenous forest that changes with the seasons; in winter dry leaves cover the ground and the shapes of branches are visible. Come spring, a faint green tinge touches the trees like a haze that, in days, becomes a new burst of leaves and the birds' early morning dawn chorus starts.

Schools bring classes, home schooling mums have workshops, poets and poetry readings take place here, there are book launches, and overnighters come to patch their battered psyches together. Individuals, in workshop conditions, get help in the various genre. And the holidays bring the children in for their workshop classes.

My junior webmaster and Vlad Buzdugan, who are preparing to be comperes on our first Kidzone Internet radio show, met with webmaster Allan Jackson to work out the programme.

Small journalists come to learn reporting for their schools to add news to our KidZone Gazette. The Manor Gardens original writers, now big pre-teens in grade 6, still come for the occasional writing session, which includes rushing around the grounds, smelling, listening and even writing in the swimming pool, taking after their mentor!

Launches that take place three or four times a year here are wonderful. The book bar has a high circular counter for food and fruit juices and wine. The outside patio is roofed with sloping wooden slats. New authors invite their nearest and dearest to listen to them read a small piece from their *own* illustrated books which they then autograph.

The whole atmosphere of excitement and pleasure is tangible as students who have diligently come to Wednesday afternoon writing lessons may have a chance to go public with books they particularly want to share.

Brenda Ueland's lovely quote is so true: "Writing is a generosity of the spirit". This *sharing* is what writing is all about. The books are available to see as media books, class readers, or simply as books to entertain. They can also be viewed on our internet domain, http://www.umsinsi.com and may be ordered from anywhere around the world using our internet shopping facilities.

UmSinsi house is a retreat. It can accommodate writing groups of twelve people sharing, or six in single rooms. There is no television. It is a spiritual place for writers to get in touch with their real selves. Lap desks provide a chance to sit amidst the trees or outside, where bird song and the wind in the trees are the only sounds. There is plenty of table space for artists to illustrate their work.

With our method of creative writing, it is important to read back and groups meet after writing sessions. A course puts a writer in touch with creativity and the knowledge that he or she “can.” Then the rest can be done from home or anywhere that the person lives.

## Chapter 33: KidZone Expands 1999

The green envelope was neatly typed and addressed to me. I opened it. The letter inside was also on green paper, and also neatly typed.

It read:

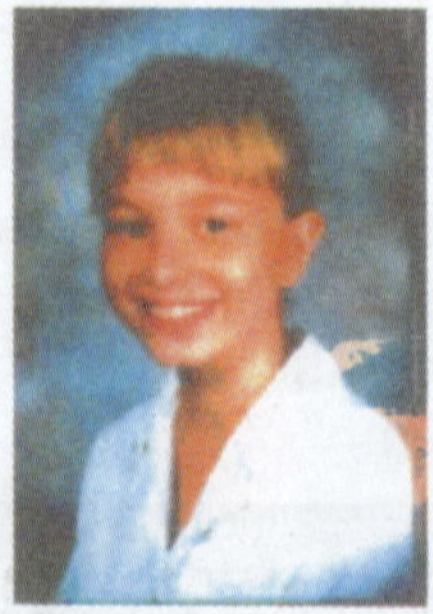

> Dear Mrs Keats
> I am eleven years of age, and I have read your book, *Creative Writing for Children in Four Easy Lessons*. I have done all the exercises. Please can you tell me - how does one become an author?
> Stefnie Perlman

I was so touched with this letter by this young girl. I looked in the phone book and found the surname, checked the address and then I rang her mother and invited Stefnie, a pupils at Gordon Road Girls' School, Durban, to be my guest at a holiday workshop that I was having later that week

That is how I first met Stefnie. On the way home, she told me that she had found our internet writers' site (called Arena, with hints for writers, which I had begun in 1996,) to be "too adult."

*That means it's boring*, I thought, remembering my granddaughter's reaction to my adult-viewpoint children's story. Stefnie suggested an attractive colourful site that children would love. She could create a web page for me, for free, and be my webmaster. This, at eleven years of age!

I was so touched with the offer that I checked it out with my Webmaster, Allan Jackson. He agreed to do the background work necessary for such a site.

"Okay," I said. "That's a deal."

On the way to our next meeting, Stefnie said, "We could have a chat room too, so we can chat to each other. I checked the idea with my brother and he thinks it's great."

"How old is your brother?" I asked, imagining him to be about fifteen.

"Four," replied Stefnie.

I said nothing...but my mind processed the information. (I later found out that he was three and a half!) Then Stefnie, Allan and I had a meeting to put some ideas together.

Two weeks later, we had a second meeting. By now Allan had the technology sorted out, Stefnie had written her pieces and done a design of what she wanted. I had collected the first story by Laura Moores in Grade 5 at Benjamin Pine Junior School, and a poem from Liza Wang of Pietermaritzburg Girls' High School. Vlad Buzdugan of Park View Primary School had written the first instalment of the boys' interactive book, and Lesley Connolly of Manor Gardens Primary School had done the girls' first instalment. A third meeting checked to see that everything was working properly.

Next came the launch at Edgewood Training College which was attended by media teachers, pupils and young writers. The SABC TV-2-Nite team was also there and we were on television that evening. The television interviewer asked me, "Isn't this a very responsible thing for an eleven-year-old to be doing on her own?"

My answer was, "My webmaster has set up a means for me to edit her work on my computer from my home. He can also edit her work. So she has the support of two adults."

The next question was, "Where are you heading?"

My answer was, "An online school newspaper that kids could read. Schools can e-mail to me their school news and activities. This will make for good communication between kids at different schools, teach them about using computers and the Internet, and also it will train young journalists. And we'll create some electronic post-cards they can send each other."

The site started well and Stefnie had many visits daily telling her what a "cool" site it was.

I couldn't wait to start the newspaper and e-mailed Allan to that effect. He e-mailed me back and suggested I get together some young journalists from the schools and give them some lessons in journalism and tell them what we would be needing for the site. We would need material for a front page story, social events, sport, and a special Junior Primary corner. And an "Out and About" for weekends, holidays, and out-of-school hours.

So, for the next few Monday afternoons, media teachers and junior school "journalists" came to creative freewriting sessions.

Grade 3, I imagined, was far too young to write for a newspaper. Wrong again! Sixteen children from La Lucia Junior Primary school arrived with their media teacher, Mrs Sheryl Gane, for creative journalism. I had done sessions at their school so they were not newcomers to right-brained closing of eyes and writing to music.

"What do you find in a newspaper?" I asked.

Answers. "Lost and found" "Social." "Sport" "Entertainment." "For sale."

"What is the purpose of a newspaper?"

'To communicate."

"And," I said, "it also depends on who is reporting because the same thing that happens can seem different when two people from opposite sides or teams write about it. Now let's have more ideas of what your school paper could have in it."

'Jokes, cartoons, camp outs, school plays." They were involved. I was pleased to see that they had books of unlined paper.

"Now this is creative work. Don't worry about spelling punctuation and grammar. There are three things to do. Are you comfy…?" and I was off.

Amazingly good work is e-mailed to me. Brett Sibson in Grade 6 at Manor Gardens Primary School was the first contributor. More stories came from Gordon Road Girls School and from Benjamin Pine Primary School.

So one month after KidZone started, KidZone Gazette was launched, with several Junior Primary News items as well. Here are two of the contributions.

**Netball & Soccer Tournament**
**Faye Irvine Grade 3 La Lucia Junior Primary**

On Saturday it was a Netball Tournament (for girls) and Soccer (for boys). It was at Atholton in Umhlanga Rocks. I played for the Girls U8A team for LLJP.

When I got there I wanted to buy candy-floss, but my mom said I must wait until my first game was over. Sure enough she gave me R2,00 for candy-floss. It was delicious.

Our next game was in 20 minutes so I explored the school. Between games I had some interesting treats such as foxy-snax, hot chips and sweets. I played GA which helps GS to shoot. Well what can I say.... It was fun!

For your delight, here is seven-year-old Kineshta Pillay's news contribution.. Not one word of what she wrote has been changed as I typed it out from the book she wrote it in.

**Market Day 22 September 99**
**Kineshta Pillay Grade 2**
**Parkside Primary School, Malvern**

Today is Market Day. I can't believe this could happen. I am a bit nervous at first but then I am okay. My things are getting finished quickly. Our market is outside the hall.

I am selling:

| | |
|---|---|
| Packet with 4 fudges | R1,00 |
| 1 Butterfly clip | 60c |
| I bracelet | 50c |
| I Necklace | R2,00 |

Market day is not for earning money. We are working with money now, so Market day is here so we can work out our customers' change. I bought the beads for the necklace and bracelet for R14,00. I also bought condensed milk for the fudge which was R3,75 for one tin.

It started to drizzle when we began but soon it stopped and the sun is coming. It is such a lovely day.

Our next exciting development is a one-hour radio show to be compered by Stefnie and Vlad Buzdugan. They are working out a programme that will include interviews and popular songs, and which will be an interesting hour for young writers. Stefnie's eyes shone when she heard that Rob Fisher (previously our web host at Club Internet) would be sponsoring our first one-hour programme.

## Chapter 34 : LitNet Interview

In my e-mail one day I received the start of a correspondence with Izak de Vries of LitNet, an online literary journal to be found at http://www.litnet.co.za.

Izak had just got a copy of Joanna Reid's book, *"An Adventure of Nellie and Bobby."*

"Too beautiful," came the verdict. "Will you agree to be interviewed for LitNet? We'll interview Joanna as well."

Joanna's book, published by umSinsi Press eighteen months ago for Manor Gardens Primary School at their second launch, had somehow reached Izak.

I wasn't surprised. These little books get all around the world as proud parents send them off to friends and relations.

I am aware that people are interested in my activities. That is because so many people would love to write, or publish, but don't know how to get started. Maybe this book, which includes Izak's interview, will help to break their blocks as it has done for many others.

(Replying to my question as to what LitNet was, Izak replied, "LitNet started in January 1999 as small site dedicated to Afrikaans literature, but it has grown into a virtual community with twenty-six different subsites. The focus is now shifting to multilingualism with Xhosa and English sites the first to grow on the infrastructure created by the Afrikaans site.") His questions are followed by my answers which are in italics.

**Q**. Who is this person that is "so in love with" the writings of the little ones that she has decided to make a living out of it?

***A.*** *At first I missed the point that this meant **me**, because I don't think of what I am doing as "making a living." Then I gave him what I thought he needed, all of which is in chapter 25.*

**Q.** You are a tutor and a publisher. As a tutor, you work with adults and children alike. Let us split these issues for the sake of clarity and start with your visits to schools, which is how I got to know about you. If a teacher asks you: "What are you going to do with my kids?" what would your answer be?

**A.** *I only go to schools which allow me to start with a teachers' workshop, and in this I explain the "why's" of the process. They also proceed, in my workshops, to do exactly what the children are going to do. This means they know what I am going to do with their kids!*

**Q.** You also teach adults. Is the approach the same?

**A.** *I am a teacher myself with a university degree and taught at both junior and high school. I have studied all writing genres for forty years, and though I use a similar approach, I change the method to suit the genre, and also to suit the adult and his or her requirements. I go much deeper with adults.*

**Q.** About your role as a publisher - I am burning to ask you: how do you do it? The big publishing houses are retrenching staff, they weigh their options very carefully before publishing children's books, and here you are, producing a large number of titles in full colour? I mean, what is your secret?

**A.** *I work very very hard and know my craft inside out.*

**Q.** You tell the kids that you are a magician, does this have anything to do with it?

**A.** *Anybody who takes "nothing" (or words and imaginative ideas) and creates "something" (a lovely story with beautiful illustrations for others to read) IS a magician. My teaching enables most students to become "magicians" themselves.*

**Q**. Your approach to writing classes is a "non-judgemental" one. What does that mean?

**A**. *It means that the people partaking in a workshop benefit from sincere audience response better if they are not criticised. It also means that, though I am a teacher, I run teacherless classes, the student being his own critic.*

**Q**. "But," our imaginary teacher asks: "What about spelling, grammar and the like?"

**A**. *My method of writing that comes before reading means that writers will want to spell better and be better at grammar because they have become interested in writing. Interest leads to attention, leads to learning. My system comes from within, and is not an "imposed from without" system.*

**Q**. How much do you, the editor, change the text before it gets published?

**A**. *I am a purist. Very little. We want the child or the writer's voice, not the grammar check of the computer.*

**Q**. A part of your philosophy is to stimulate interest in a book-culture, something this country sorely lacks. How, do you think, can you and I get the average Afrikaans speaking kid on the farm, the average soapy-watching adult in the suburbs, or the average herd-boy in the Transkei to appreciate books?

**A**. *By my method, which is a "I want to write, I like it doing it, and I want to read my friend's story. Now I want to read library books, and oh, boy! I've found what fun learning can be!" method.*

**Q**. Is your system in line with Outcomes Based Education?

**A**. *As children not only learn to write but to put a*

*book together and to become professionals where writing and reporting are concerned, and also could become entrepeneurs by selling the books, I know our system is exactly what the Outcomes Based Education system is all about.*

*What is more, the choice by our Durban Departments of Education and Culture of sixty-eight of our books that sponsors could donate to children as classroom readers for classroom collections means that we meet the Outcomes Based Education system very well.*

*Headmasters have said to me, "We have been told to work from within, outwards, but we don't know how to do it."*

*I have fully-trained one right-brained teacher, Jabulani Hlabangane, who is ready to teach in rural areas and townships. He is half my age, and can go where I cannot go. He was a teacher of street children in the literacy department of the Ark Christian Academy in Durban but now is an umSinsi teacher. So we hope that this minute start can spiral and bring about a literate country, and a literate sub-Saharan Africa!*

*Optimistic, aren't we?*

## Chapter 35: The Biter Bit

I knew I had to write this book but it seemed such a mammoth task and there was so much to go in that I didn't know how to start.

I remembered that it was at the writers' weekend in Johannesburg that the title unexpectedly came. *Dancing Pencils,* I had thought, watching them write. It was also at that workshop that I realised that I so badly wanted to write this book - the standard of writing, the depth and sincerity were all so much what writing is about that I knew the time for the birth of the book was very near.

That night, Dee, Julian, Tony, Penny, Carol and I had chatted in Dee's lounge. Mostly it was about writing, which is a never-ending topic for writers. After they had gone, and I was in bed, I found that I couldn't sleep. I remembered those were the signs of old. This was the book wanting to get out. Labour pains, of a sort.

I had put on the light that night and had branched the book. Even if I just wrote what we did at the workshop that weekend, I'd have a book, I thought. Satisfied, I put off the light and fell asleep.

Now that I was back at home, it seemed it was a false labour. This book still didn't know how to get written.

I had received e-mails from writers whose creative side, the fiction writer in them, had been fired by the course. That was wonderful for them but still no book of mine had begun to be written. I was in despair and walked around the house with a hangdog look.

"Whatever is the matter with you?" asked my husband, an observant Virgo.

"I can't think how to do this book," I moaned.

"Just write it. Start free-writing like you tell us all to do."

My own medicine was being given back to me. I tried

that, but it wasn't enough to get me right-brained.

I was next door at night at umSinsi House and the light above the barbecue was shining in the forest. And the sky was pinkly clouded. There was no moon that I could see. How can these people access their right brains and not me? I asked myself. I must believe in myself, believe in my book, see people of all kinds reading this. Because it is for all kinds of creative people.

I came home and, remembering my rules about not stopping writing for ten minutes, I freewrote as follows, "Let it go go go go - up up and freewrite for ten minutes - some kind of bug came in the window and is in my painting basket now. Let it go go go go and shut my eyes and write - shut my eyes and write. You're doing just the same. Not allowing the right brain its space, it could want to do things very differently. Let me ask it. *"Right brain, how does one write a best seller everyone wants to read? Everyone, from teenagers to oldies."* The right brain is your treasure trove. The place where your wealth is stored."

And *then* I remembered. It was only a month ago that I had been interviewed by a Sunday newspaper. After the interview, the photographer was looking for the shot he wanted to take. It was a dull day and we walked through the winter forest crunching our way through the dried leaves that covered the ground.

"There's no sun," said the photographer. "This isn't the place for the picture."

They tried me peering through some sprays of brightly coloured bougainvillea but that's a picture for the young and beautiful. The man was in despair.

"Where do you write?" he asked at last.

"I used to have a hammock in the trees. I wrote my first book there," I said. "After that, I took to writing on an airbed on the pool."

I pointed to a bright pink air bed on the flawless blue pool. "I like writing like that, my feet trail in the water and

I move from the physical world to one of my own creation very easily."

The photographer had perked up. "Won't you pose for us?" he said, moving towards the pool.

"Why pose?" I said. "I'll show you what I do."

I kicked off my shoes and with a pencil and a pad of paper, floated off into the pool, long skirt getting wet. (The photograph is on the back cover of this book.)

Just doing that brought back to mind that this was how I *really* liked writing. I had my answer to my present problem in remembering back to that interview. I knew how I could write this book! My right brain had slipped in the answer.

Despite a slight nip in the air, it wasn't long before I was on the airbed and the same feeling of relaxation overtook me that I saw in my other writers. My pencil began to move on the paper. The start of this book just came out exactly as it is under chapter 2 called Dancing Pencils. Like a skein of wool, once the beginning started to come out, the rest would just follow.

In five days I had written thirty thousand words. I wrote in bed, I wrote at night. I wrote on the computer, with the monitor switched off, or with the font on white. I slept, woke and wrote. In ten days I was up to forty-eight thousand words. The baby was out, the waters had broken.

"Mrs Aughrabies Falls Morrison," my husband called me.

I knew what had come out needed refining and polishing; it was a frightful mess but I knew a huge joy. My right-brained method works! It works for others *and* it works for me!

And with writing as a companion, there is no need to ever be bored, or lonely. Here is one true friend, your true self, you can trust to help you write whatever it is that you wish to do. With your right brain slipping away from the control of the left brain, all kinds of delights come from your pen onto the paper.

Control, the home of the left brain, assumes that you with your relatively small ego do *have* the power to *be* in control. This cannot be! Just take the sun that rises each morning on cue and the stars in the heavens and take heart that there is a tremendous control over the universe and the heavens but that it has nothing to do with a person and their ego.

It is when one learns to let go, to give up control, that there is hope - because then the whole knowledge of the universe becomes accessible and with it, many more benefits than would happen if control were the key issue.

In fact, true security is only the ability to live serenely with insecurity. Be happy in the moment. The other way leads to fears of all kinds. Losing money, face, possessions, family, health being just some of the factors to alter things.

To be left-brained, means to have the critic on the look-out. The left brain divides, and is the cause of much trouble. "Thor the Thunderer" in Nordic mythology was not able to cross the Bifrost bridge - in the most significant passage I have ever read, I understood so much. Thor was the cause of misery and suffering in the world of thought that it had created and it also chained and kept the world a prisoner. The subtleties of the right brain use were too amazing to really write about. Here the strangest war of all took place. If one believed the words of the left brain and the actions that were a result, then one became chained to those negativities. Denying them was not the answer either. They were facts and had been caused by the left brain.

But what then was the answer?

The answer was the subtlest of all. T*o know by simply knowing* toppled the left brain, and tapped the vast resources of the right brain, tapped into the universe and higher benefits and positive realities occurred.

It was Einstein who said the imagination was more important than knowledge.

There is a tremendous power in your imagination. You will find, in your writing, that you are there, where you are imagining, and the colours, smells, shapes and sounds are real to you even though they are in your head.

It's so real that you can feel the cool breeze, smell the scent of pine trees, hear the rustle of dried leaves and see glimmers on the water. If you practise this work of the imagination, controlled imagination, you will find your answers to writing.

Like osmosis, this can make for a better world. The lives one touches can be better for one's presence.

Surely in a world destroying itself because of negativity and gloom, which shuns the good things just because they *are* the good things, we might pause long enough to give the right brain, the gently enormous all-knowing creative partner, enough encouragement to allow it to bring forth its wealth and its wisdom?

## Chapter 36 : The ideal : literacy and being literate

Being literate can mean a good job that you enjoy, a warm and happy home, travel if you wish, and a good education for your children with a chance to give them culture, which always *costs.*

Clichéd, perhaps, but the truth is, this *is* the truth.

Take illiteracy, on the other hand.

Thieving, arrogance, *smart-Alecs*, ruthlessness, con men, gangsters, violence, crime, always on the move, dodging the authorities, not there when the sheriff comes. Does this sound like the life we imagined when we were first growing up?

If you have had the chance to grow up with lovely things around you, and in a warm and caring environment, this may just sound like words to you.

But if you have grown up with *shebeens* on either side of the road, drunken voices, police sirens; if you have been scared at the noise and the shouting and the sobbing and even the dying, you will know that what I am saying is real. It does happen, not to mention starvation and the lack of finance to deal with grave matters of health.

If this frightens you, if you are sensitive enough to look at what I am saying, please know that this book holds the answer to the problem of literacy. I am a teacher myself, with a university degree and a university education diploma, and I have moved about in the company of teachers a great deal. I like teachers enormously.

I love education and know no greater joy than being in a school with children, hundreds of children, but I enjoy it now, in my particular way. This is simply to give children (and teachers) a chance to get in touch with their reality, with their inner being, with the part of them that moves across to the right brain, the home of music, religion and the higher finer things in life.

Know, then, that the negative destructive ways of society are easy. The higher finer kind and good things are more in hiding and you need to search for them, but when you have found them you will hang onto them for they are the real things in life, the knowledge of one's own divinity, you could call it.

What I am saying is that there is a choice of what we do and how we spend our lives. And that choice starts early with the decision to be literate, or not.

The choice to remain illiterate may not be a conscious one. It may be a rebellion, a resistance, and all the kind people who wish to impose this wonderful thing, literacy, on others, mean well, but that's not the way to do it. You have to make people *want* it, and the way you make them want it is in exactly the way that I have told in these pages. If you have been reading carefully, you will have discovered how.

I can vouch for it that every child in every school wants to have a peaceful quiet atmosphere in which to let the treasures of his imagination out on paper. Schools are told to get the child to bring the work out from within but it's meaningless words to them. What does this actually mean?

It means - and I spell this out very clearly - that writing comes before reading, and that the interest in spelling will follow. This leads to better writing, more reading, better spelling, interest in learning, and so towards literacy. School becomes a pleasant place where teachers don't walk around with small canes or rulers to whack the disruptive person in the class.

It will be only the few who will take what I say and do something with it, but we have to start somewhere. It is osmosis, and the emphasis on the good, the writing; your writing, the books the children are writing; all will foster the dreams of a better life.

I talk a lot with teachers and headmasters, who admit that the left brain has a great control over them. Some who would like to write, are eager to learn how to drop this control, if only for the sake of allowing their great sleeping partner in with its insights and writing ability where the correct image is always apt, and where truths come that would otherwise not be accessible.

So - if a person has a good education, this right-brained work will bring out wonderful writing. Yet again, think of someone who is just starting out with English as his or her second language, and who is getting dispirited for being in constant trouble because of bad spelling or word usage.

Can you imagine his or her excitement if he or she is allowed just to write anything! If it is not very good, and he or she is praised for the story, for the imaginative use of words, for the real writing (nothing plastic) can you see that a warm feeling will grow? If this child comes from a background of violence and poverty, all the more he or she needs encouragement.

We need schools where teachers can learn right brained non-judgmental, non-critical release of creativity: we know that all creativity, inventions, ideas, and all the great new innovations we need for the world of the 2000's, comes from being in touch with the right brain; that part of us that is so sensitive that it goes into hiding when criticized.

The thought of a society of left-brained methodical straight-line thinkers who do as they are told is gloomy, but with them as a backup to the geniuses resulting from the right brain explosion of creativity would mean a wonderful, exciting, progressive and positive society.

Remember, it's a whole brain we're are after, but the process of a whole brain needs to go the way in which this book tells you.

In conclusion, this is just a snippet of all that has been happening, is happening, and is going to happen for writers here. Our country is badly in need of writers and journalists; we haven't a proper literature. We have fascinating people and fascinating cultures. So - if you *want* to write stories, poetry, articles or a book and you feel you have something important to say, then know you can just *start*. Remember to get right-brained by becoming still and activating the imagination. Remember that you only need to have the tip of the iceberg along with the desire to write. Study this book, it holds many vital clues to your success as a writer. Know that writing is hard work and it's lonely, but know that you will get all the help you need.

Remember serendipity, and look out for the clues to your direction. Ask questions, and answer them with your non-dominant hand! Keep following the clues your right brain brings to you and you *will* make it happen for yourself.

And as the children of today are the adults of tomorrow, what better way than to start off by unlocking their creativity, and encouraging them to write?

# BIBLIOGRAPHY


*Becoming a Writer,* Dorothea Brande, 1984, Papermac
ISBN 0 333 34573 4
*The Right Brain Experience,* Marilee Zdenek, 1986, Corgi
ISBN 0 552 12623 3
*If you Want to Write,* Brenda Ueland, 1991, Element Books
ISBN 1 85230 215 1
*Writing on Both Sides of the Brain,* Henriette Klauser, 1987, Harper San Francisco
ISBN 0 06 254490 X
*Writing With Power,* Peter Elbow:,1981, OUP
ISBN 0 19 502913 5
*Writing Without Teachers,* Peter Elbow, 1973, OUP
ISBN 0 19 501679 3
*Writing down the Bones,* Natalie Goldberg, 1986, Shambhala Publications
ISBN 0 87773 375 9
*Guide to Fiction Writing,* Phyllis Whitney, 1984, Poplar Press Ltd
ISBN 0 907657 07 9
*The Power of Your Other Hand,* Lucia Capacchione, Newcastle Publishing Co. Inc
ISBN0-87877-130-1
*The Elements of Style,* William Strunk Jnr., MacMillan Publishing Co.
*Drawing on the Right Side of the Brain,* Betty Edwards, Fontana Paperbacks
ISBN 0-00-636602-3
*Poetry in the Making,* Ted Hughes, Faber and Faber
ISBN 0-571-08701-9
Santa Barbara Fiction Writers Guide, Writers' Digest Books
ISBN 0-89879-395-5
*Use your Head,* Tony Buzan, Ariel Books
ISBN 0-563-16552-9
*The Way to Write for children,* Joan Aiken, 1982, Elm Tree Books
ISBN 0-241-10745-8
*The Road Less Travelled,* M. Scott Peck, An Arrow NewAge Book
ISBN 0-09097270-4
*Self Unfoldment BY Disciplines of Realization,* Manley Palmer Hall Philosophical Research Society
*The Magic of Believing,* Claude M Bristol, 1948, Prentice-Hall Inc,
*The Buddhist way of Action,* Christmas Humphreys, Mandala Edition ,1977
Unwin Paperbacks ISBN 0-04-294100-8

**Umsinsi Press Creative Writing Books**

*Creative Writing in Four Easy Lessons*, Felicity Keats, 1996, UmSinsi Press, ISBN 0-620-19693-9
*Creative Writing for Children in Four Easy Lessons*, Felicity Keats, *1997*, UmSinsi Press, ISBN 1-919721-26-6
*Introducing Journalism in Four Easy Lessons*, Felicity Keats, *1997*, UmSinsi Press, ISBN 1-919721-22-3
*Creative Novel Writing* , Felicity Keats, 1999, UmSinsi Press
ISBN 1-86900-176-X
*The Magic Tortoise*, Felicity Keats, 1999, UmSinsi Press
ISBN 1-86900-177-x
*Creative Short Story Writing*, Felicity Keats, 1999, UmSinsi Press
ISBN 1-86900-178-8
*Imagination S-T-R-E-C-H*, Felicity Keats, 1999, UmSinsi Press
ISBN 1-86900-179-6

**Other umSinsi Press publications mentioned in this book**

*Moments with Radiance*, Charl Fregona, 1996, UmSinsi Press
ISBN 1-919721-01-0
*Handspun: Words and Images*, Elizabeth Vels, 1998, UmSinsi Press
ISBN 1-919721-02-9
Collaborations : a book of South African art and poetry, 1999, UmSinsi Press, ISBN 1-86900-29-X
*South African Short Stories Volume 1: Sundowners*, 1995, UmSinsi Press
ISBN 0-620-19419-7
*South African Short Stories Volume 2: Cadences*, 1995, UmSinsi Press
ISBN 0-620-19692-0
South African Short Stories Volume 3: Roots, 1997, UmSinsi Press
ISBN 1-919721-17-7
South African Short Stories Volume 4: Voices, 1998, UmSinsi Press
ISBN 1-919721-78-9
*Mindscapes of the Nineties*, Dee Andrew, *1998*, UmSinsi Press
ISBN 1-919721-77-0
*The Cat Witches of Stinkfeet*, Gillian Gorman, *1998*, UmSinsi Press
ISBN 1-919721-72-X
*The Big Green Mysterious Place*, Genna Chorn, 1997,UmSinsi Press
ISBN 1-919721-20-7
*The Adventures of Nellie and Bobby*, Joanna Reid, 1998, UmSinsi Press
ISBN 1-919721-48-7
*The Dogopillar*, Jessie-Lee Redding, UmSinsi Press
ISBN 1-86900-158-3

*The Zebra with No Stripes*, Sian Jones, UmSinsi Press, 1999,
ISBN 1-86900-144-3
*Mãe*, Ester Lee, *1996*, UmSinsi Press
ISBN 0-620-20342-0
*That Old Stove*, Felicity Keats and Genna Chorn, 1995, UmSinsi Press
ISBN 0-620-19835-4
*The Life of Samual and his brother Blue*, Rachel Baasch, 1996, UmSinsi Press
ISBN 1-919721-12-6
*Sasha's World*, Loren Johnston, 1996, UmSinsi Press
ISBN 1-919721-10-X
*The Adventures of Abby and Tabby*, Giovanna Cowley, 1996, UmSinsi Press
ISBN 1-919721-13-4
*My Cat on Holiday*, Lucy Sessions, 1996, UmSinsi Press
ISBN 1-919721-11-8
*Samson's Surprise*, Jabulani Hlabangane, 1997, UmSinsi Press
ISBN 1-919721-19-3
*Themba's Hope*, Jabulani Hlabangane, 1997, UmSinsi Press
1SBN 1-919721-44-4
*An Adventure of Nelly and Bobby*, Joanna Reid, 1998, UmSinsi Press
ISBN 1-919721-48-7
*2 Cats and 12 Poems*, Eva Jackson, 1999, UmSinsi Press
ISBN 1-86900-147-8
*Dimension Arthropod Terra*, Vlad Buzdugan, *1998*, UmSinsi Press
ISBN 1-86900-015-3
*Wanda's Glowing "Wish" Shoes*, Rowan McAllister, 1998, UmSinsi Press,
ISBN 1-86900-082-X
*The Story of Rex*, Nomfundo Radebe, 1998, UmSinsi Press
ISBN 1-86900-098-6
*The Bravest Dog in the World*, Avinash Singh, 1998, UmSinsi Press
ISBN 1-919721-
*'n Vlooi se Lewe, Aai!* Melissa Beukman, 1998, UmSinsi Press
ISBN 1-86900-008-0
*Poems*, Liza Wang,1998, Umsinsi Press
ISBN 1-86900-012-9
*Another Volume of Poems*, Liza Wang, 1999, UmSinsi Press
ISBN 1-86900-125-7
*Flappies Red die Dag*, Nadine Komen, 1998, UmSinsi Press
ISBN 1-86900-007-2
*Alien Adventure*, Nadine Komen, 1999, Umsinsi Press
ISBN 1-86900-126-5
*The Bad Dream Spider and Other Stories*, Jade Fernley, UmSinsi Press
ISBN 1-919721-50-9

**Other Felicity Keats publications by Umsinsi press**

*A Piece of Jasper*, 1998, ISBN 0-620-20341-2
*Rose October:*, 1998, ISBN 1-919721-55-X
*The Moshwahs, 1998*, ISBN 1-919721-05-3
*The Birth of a Queen*, 1997, ISBN 1-919721-29-0
*For You and for Me:* ISBN 1-919721-35-5
*The weatherman's mistake:* ISBN 1-919721-24-*x*

**Felicity Keats publications by Tafelberg Press**

*The Wild Swarm*, ISBN 06-240-27382
*Die Wilde Swerm* ISBN 06-240-27384
*Rudolphs' Valley*, 1991, ISBN 0-624-02939-5